David Thulstrup

David Thulstrup

A Sense of Place

Sophie Lovell

Introduction

One of the things I most love about my work are the moments of anticipation – sitting in a car, travelling somewhere new, when I am waiting to encounter a new place for the first time. Then I love the time spent moving through that new place, on high alert and with all my senses open – evaluating the trees, the soil, the stone, the movement of the sun and the touch of the wind. It doesn't take long for me to begin to imagine a new building there, or the transformation of an existing volume.

This sense of place is at the very heart of each project that I work on, and once the place is established in my mind and imagination, I can go on to build around it. My sense of place is an awareness of the journey and process: changing, evolving, growing, and becoming more refined as I progress from project to project.

I daydream about my projects today in much the same way as I did whilst sitting on a church pew on Sundays with my family as a child. I would perch in that huge sacral space daydreaming about different ways of transforming it, giving it a new purpose, function, materiality, and volumes. In the beginning, I relied on my intuition to realise and articulate my projects. Now, after fourteen years of making it my career, I can, within my projects, verbalise what I am after far better and translate what is essentially a purely sensory awareness and personal creative process with clarity and accuracy into both words, images and physical structures.

I have reached a place of creative clarity, where I feel ready to collect some of my projects to date together as a body of work in their own right, in order to share them and to share the path I took to achieve them so far. Today I am busier than ever before with so many new projects and it has helped me too, as I move forward, to spend time gathering and reflecting upon what I hope has been but the first stage of my creative journey in this book. I'm so proud of every one of the projects featured here, and just as proud of my team who have worked so hard with me on them. I am so grateful too to my clients, past, present, and future, for trusting me and my vision to help them create their special places.

David Thulstrup

Learning to Walk
Knopskydende

"Out of the blue, I was approached by a client who said they had bought an old farmhouse up in the north of Denmark and asked me if I would come and have a look. He told me the address and it was my old childhood home."

Hans David Thulstrup was born in Hørsholm, Denmark on November 29, 1978, the youngest of five children, to Inge Thulstrup, a nurse, and Hans Thulstrup, a family doctor. Up until he was twelve years old, David and his family lived in a large old house there, near the Øresund coast, beside a forest where he remembers playing often as a child.

In the eighteenth century, Hørsholm was famous as the site of a baroque royal summer palace, once known as the Versailles of the North, which was built in 1733 for King Christian VI and his queen, Sophie Magdalena of Denmark. However, following a scandalous royal episode involving the subsequent King Christian VII, his wife Caroline Mathilda, and the royal physician Johann Friedrich Struensee (which ended in the doctor's execution and the banishment and imprisonment of the queen), the palace was abandoned and eventually torn down in 1810. Just over a decade later, it was replaced with a more modestly proportioned Lutheran church designed by the architect Christian Frederik Hansen, who also designed Copenhagen Cathedral.

The Thulstrup family house was built on top of the former underground ice store belonging to Hørsholm Palace and had views across the surrounding landscape and towards the forest. It was not a grand house but had been added to and altered over time, so it was a composite of several different annexes and extensions with, unsurprisingly, an extremely large stone cellar.

For Thulstrup, this childhood home had considerable influence on the aesthetic sense he would later develop as a designer. "I think having grown up and lived in an environment like that, that is where my passion for materiality comes from. It was not until recently that I became aware of how my senses of material, colour, space, warmth and comfort were sculpted around that home," he says.

He has vivid memories of the grey Greenlandic marble floors, dark wood panelling and exposed wooden beams of the interior, as well as the moulded plaster inserts above the doorframes and the four fireplaces. "Thinking about the interior of my childhood home again", he adds, "has also made me realise that I have always had an issue with the general perception of Scandinavian interiors being non-material, minimalistic spaces with pale wooden floors and white walls, because I have never lived like that; I grew up surrounded by massive materiality." He remembers strongly-coloured rooms with dark green or yellow walls, black gloss-painted doors, and window frames, and, interestingly, the kitchen was painted black too.

> "I remember the kitchen very well. It was in one of the extensions and had low wooden ceilings, black walls and a huge wooden dining table built around a column. It looked out onto a conservatory that had big glass windows, which covered two whole sides of the house. Because we were a family with five kids, there were often a lot of people at the house for dinner besides us, my parents and the old lady that looked after us when my parents were at work. If just one of my four siblings had friends over after school, there could be ten or more people at the table."

Thulstrup also remembers his parents having an eclectic mix of furnishings from Verner Panton lamps and Poul Kjærholm chandeliers to classical furniture pieces and objects they had inherited from their own parents. "There was an old communist plaster sculpture that came with the house," he adds, "and in the middle of the conservatory was a fish pool carved into the marble floor."

Growing up, Thulstrup was very much the baby of the family. His eldest two brothers, Michael and Peter, are sixteen and twelve years older, respectively, and the twins, Thomas and Therese, are eight years older. His parents were both Catholic converts, and the Thulstrup children had a Catholic upbringing with church visits every Sunday – not to the aforementioned local Lutheran church but to one of Denmark's few Roman Catholic places of worship, St. Theresa's, some 20 kilometres

(12 miles) away. Thulstrup remembers it as having a very simple interior. "It was a huge, empty space with a cross on the wall." It was in this place of worship on Sundays that he began to discover his love of spatial design as well as learn to sit still, listen and observe. "In church, I learned how to reflect and notice things. I would be constantly decorating and remodelling the space in my mind. Even when I was young, I thought a lot about what something could become," he says. "By my early teens, I began to have an awareness of this ability with my imagination. It was not linked specifically to design or architecture at the time, but to volumes and rooms and what functionality you could put into them."

By the time he was twelve, Thulstrup's four siblings had all finished high school and left home. The big house was sold and Thulstrup moved with his parents into a modern two-storey apartment located nearby on the coast. They moved once again to an apartment in Copenhagen when Thulstrup was around sixteen, although he continued to attend his high school, Rungsted Gymnasium, which involved a twenty-minute train ride back up to Hørsholm every day.

At high school, Thulstrup focused on maths and physics, and, for the first time, had a chance to study something called "design". Alongside the basics of drawing and colour theory, there was also something called "design evaluation," during which the class had to write short essays about a chosen design object. Thulstrup chose to write about Philippe Starck's Dr. Kiss toothbrush designed in 1996 for Officina Alessi. "It was wavy and had a stand, almost like a feather quill standing in an inkpot. I thought that was the coolest thing back then" he says. Thulstrup's design interest grew from there, and he began to focus on product design and fashion.

After finishing school at eighteen, Thulstrup went to work at Le Saint Jacques, a brasserie in Copenhagen. The restaurant was owned by the French chef Daniel Letz, who was the first chef in Denmark to earn a Michelin star. Letz also trained Thulstrup's second eldest brother, Peter, who was a chef. After a few months, Peter called David from Paris – where he now owned a well-known restaurant of his own, La Petite Sirène de Copenhague, in the 9th arrondissement – to say their au pair had quit unexpectedly and to ask if Thulstrup would be interested in coming to Paris to look after his son Paul.

So in the spring of 1998, Thulstrup moved to Paris. After a few enjoyable months au-pairing for his nephew, he started looking into foundation courses for architecture and fashion, and he was accepted at a small private school near the Bastille, Atelier Clouet, to complete an *année préparatoire*. He enjoyed his year there a great deal despite the challenge of having to master a new language in the process: "Everything was in French, so it took me about three months before I really understood what they were talking about," he says, "at first, I mostly watched the others and did what they were doing: If they were painting a rabbit, I painted a rabbit."

Atelier Clouet taught a classic foundation course. The students were all there for a year to create portfolios of work in order to apply for fashion, design, art or architecture colleges. Their days were filled with exercises in a range of creative media and disciplines, including line drawing, wire-frame sculpture, cardboard model-making, *croquis* and colour exercises. One of Thulstrup's favourite aspects of the course was that every other week the students all had to go and see a particular exhibition and then write a report. Growing up in a large family back home meant that going to an exhibition was something that happened once or twice a year at most. Thulstrup remembers his parents taking the five siblings occasionally to Ordrupgaard and Louisiana or to classical concerts, but being exposed to art museums on a very regular basis was completely new to him. "It opened my eyes to so many great artists and so much great architecture that I don't think I would have experienced in Copenhagen at the time." Two of the exhibitions he remembers having a particular impact on him were an Anish Kapoor show at Chapelle Saint-Louis de la Salpêtrière and Christian Boltanski at Palais de Tokyo.

By the time Thulstrup finished his foundation year, he had begun to focus on architecture and interiors, so he applied to the Royal Danish Academy of Architecture and the Danish Design School. At that time, acceptance at the architecture academy was more dependent on school exam grades and Thulstrup was not offered a place. But the strength of his interiors portfolio did win him a place at the design school. So in 2000, Thulstrup moved back to Copenhagen to study spatial design at what is now known as the Royal Danish Academy of Fine Arts. Whilst he was in Paris, his parents had retired and spent most of the year in the South of France, so he was able to live in their Copenhagen apartment, which he shared with his older brother Michael, an engineer.

Design college in Denmark turned out to be very different from Thulstrup's experiences in Paris. "The school in Paris was very active, whereas, in Denmark, it was much more about sitting at a desk and studying – less practical, less doing," he says. Finding this formal design study experience very restrictive, he started to look around for something to balance it out. This was at a time before social media, when lifestyle magazines, such as *Wallpaper**, were really booming in Europe. These publications were all about visual impact and often contained numerous elaborate and creatively styled photo shoots within each issue. Thulstrup applied for a job as an intern for a freelance stylist, and before long, he was signed to Style Counsel, Denmark's leading fashion, advertising, and production agency at the time. Then, at the age of twenty-one and still in his first year of design school, Thulstrup started his own styling business and ran it for the next two years, styling interior shoots for both fashion and design productions as well as scouting locations for commercials and lifestyle magazines, such as the Danish publication *Dansk*. "I worked so hard and so much both for school and at the agency, and I loved it," he says. "It was an amazing learning experience."

One of the photographers Thulstrup worked with was Peter Krasilnikoff, whose house he ended up designing years later

with a commission that would put Thulstrup on the interior architecture map professionally. "I remember a shoot we did under the main stairs of Arne Jacobsen's Radisson SAS Royal Hotel," says Thulstrup. "It had a black marble floor, and the beautiful geometry of the staircase could just be seen in the shot. All we added was a palisander wood table and a single, simple vase." Thulstrup has never been one for too many objects, so the experience of learning about good lighting and playing in a minimal way with three-dimensions for a photographic image helped him understand the layers that create a good picture. "When you are styling for the camera, you might place a chair that looks completely off in the room, but through the frame of the lens, it is correct because you have to account for the perspective," he explains. "I still love doing that; it's why I am always at the photo shoots for all of my projects."

Thulstrup loved the fast pace, the energy and the people he encountered in the photography styling world. The experiences he had and the business connections he made during this intense time of work and study would also stand him in good stead later. Meanwhile, in his bachelor's course at college, he seemed to be muddling through. "I was not really a favourite of my teachers," he says. "They liked me because I am a nice and likeable person, but they couldn't really figure out where to place me. I always work very quietly with what I do, and I think they could not really figure out what it was exactly I did: 'Styling? What is that? It's not architecture, it's not furniture... This is supposed to be about interiors, not scenography...' I think they thought I was a little bit superficial and could not work out why I was not designing offices or kitchens." Thulstrup was clearly not made for a two-dimensional world behind a desk. He needed three or four dimensions to flourish. "I learned most when I was out in the world experiencing for myself what it means to work with light, colour, shape and objects."

Thulstrup's final bachelor's degree project was where he first brought the two worlds of his work and study together on a large scale. Through his styling work, he had made numerous manufacturing and retail contacts and had no qualms about calling them up to ask for the loan of products or materials for his degree show. The Danish bespoke wood and flooring company Dinesen was one of these contacts. He got them to sponsor the material for the centrepiece of his project: an extraordinarily long table – about twelve metres (39 ft) in length – of geometric shapes rising out of the floor, all made from Dinesen oak planks that were cut up and stuck together. Thulstrup also used his contacts with both Georg Jensen, a silver and jewellery design company, and Royal Copenhagen porcelain to borrow cutlery, glasses and tableware, which he then combined with other objects to use in the styling of his table. For Thulstrup, his degree show was about demonstrating his burgeoning skillset for creating atmosphere and telling stories in space. "I think another one of my passions – for mixing things – really developed then," he says, "putting objects like palisander plates from the 1960s together with cutlery from the 1880s and modern glass from the 2000s … the show was a huge success."

Thulstrup was not the only one to think his bachelor's project was a triumph. Rasmus Nordqvist, a friend of his who was a fashion designer at the time had an upcoming show on the Avenue des Champs-Élyseés in Paris that year and suggested using Thulstrup's installation as a centrepiece for his fashion show. So, with some help from Dinesen, Georg Jensen and Royal Copenhagen, the entire installation was shipped over and reinstalled at the Maison du Danemark for the opening and an ensuing exhibition in the summer of 2003. Martine Gram, a Danish woman who worked for Kvadrat in France and would later become a good friend – attended the show with her husband, the designer Aurélien Barbry. Barbry happened to work for the office of the architect Jean Nouvel as a member of the product design team, and he suggested that Thulstrup apply for an internship with them. Since Thulstrup was in the gap between his bachelor's and master's degrees (the stage where a practical internship was required as part of his studies), he applied for and earned a place in the interior

department at Ateliers Jean Nouvel. At the time, the head of the design department was Yves Marbrier, the former editor of *Vogue Decoration* magazine.

This opportunity provided a huge leap in work experience for Thulstrup. In the early 2000s, Jean Nouvel's architecture practice and small design studio, made up of only eight to twelve designers, was highly productive. Marbrier oversaw "whatever was not architecture." There were two teams: one for product and the other for interiors. Other design team members included Gesa Hansen, the aforementioned Aurélien Barbry and Frédéric Imbert, who were designing office furniture for Molteni's UniFor, the Less office furniture series for Fondation Cartier, a concept car for Fiat, kitchen pans for Tefal, the Steel Matte cutlery series for Georg Jensen, the Waterborn textile range for Kvadrat and more. The interiors team were working on projects that ranged from the executive offices and an auditorium in Jean Nouvel's Torre Agbar in Barcelona to the Musée du quai Branly Jacques Chirac and the Danish Radio Concert House auditorium, including fixtures and fittings, in Copenhagen, as well as an apartment building and show apartments in New York. During his time at Jean Nouvel's practice, Thulstrup worked on the projects in New York, the City Hall in Marseille, and a set of private houses in East Asia, amongst others. "He was shy, very good-tempered, and hard-working," remembers Marbrier of his former intern. "He worked with everybody and helped whoever needed help. Colours and materials were his speciality."

Where others might have taken time off after completing their degree, Thulstrup spent his summer holiday in 2003 on a course that taught the architecture drawing programme AutoCAD. Eventually, after six months of interning at Jean Nouvel's studio, he was offered a job there. He took a leave of absence from college, and ended up staying at the firm for three years – six months of which he worked in the evenings on his master's degree.

In December 2005, Thulstrup took a month off work to finish his Master of Arts degree back at the Danish Design School. For his master's project, Thulstrup chose to design a Danish restaurant interior in New York that a friend of a friend was planning to open. "It didn't happen in the end, but it did bring me my graduate degree and my first visit to New York," says Thulstrup. "The design was very much inspired by the streets and lights of the city. [The interior] was a very long, narrow space, and I think I made a high counter that stretched all through the space. The materials were steel, concrete, stone, and coloured glass – with a lot of orange." He remembers still being influenced by the work of Phillipe Starck at the time, but not so much by the formal language – as in the toothbrush design that had fascinated him at school – as Starck's "twisting of functionality with expressionistic elements."

After graduating, Thulstrup returned to working for Nouvel full-time for a while before leaving to try his hand at freelance work in Paris, but that proved to be quite a struggle so in late 2006, he decided it was time to broaden his skillset. The world of luxury retail design had caught his eye, especially the work of one interior architect: Peter Marino. "I still really loved fashion and the pace that came with it, so when I became aware of the amazing architect Peter Marino, I decided I wanted to work for him." So in his typically direct and fearless fashion, Thulstrup flew to Marino's New York offices for an interview, got the job and started with him in February 2007.

An American architect born in 1949, Peter Marino is perhaps the world's leading designer of luxury fashion stores. He started his own practice in 1978 when Andy Warhol hired him to renovate his townhouse, and since, has gone on to build a client list that includes such brands as Louis Vuitton, Armani, Zegna, Calvin Klein, Fendi and Christian Dior. He is perhaps most famous for his Chanel boutiques. So, when Thulstrup decided to try his hand at designing luxury retail interiors, he went straight to the top – and was accepted. "The work was fantastic," he recalls, "I worked in the Chanel team under Darren Nolan,

who was one of the partners who had been with Peter for many years, and he gave me pretty much free rein to explore my own creativity." This also meant that Thulstrup got to present his designs directly to Marino as well.

> "Getting that exposure to exclusivity and luxury and having the chance to develop a lot of different concepts for a specific brand was fantastic. I was left to develop and allowed to be creative; to show Peter my ideas and have that dialogue with him."

These kinds of conversations were to prove invaluable to Thulstrup when he later had his own company and team of his own. They taught him how to balance his own ideas and expectations with encouraging the creativity and imaginations of his employees.

> "That level of team dialogue is what I really learned from Peter. Another thing that I admired so much about him is that he has his own aesthetic identity but is also always open to exploring others – using new materials and ways of combining things."

It is from Marino that Thulstrup also learned to define himself through his approach rather than a specific style – always remaining adaptive to the client, the brief and the situation. Working for Marino also had parallels with working for Nouvel. "Both had teams of around one hundred people, and just like Jean, Peter had great team leaders to balance out his ideas with, but both places were quite patriarchal in terms of there being a clear leader," Thulstrup says. "It was very clear who you worked for."

Thulstrup settled in quite quickly in New York. He found a room in a two-bedroom apartment in Greenwich Village that he shared with another architect. He loved the work and thrived in the Peter Marino office, but he was very homesick for Paris and his friends. Thulstrup had previously come out whilst living in Paris in his early twenties. It was, he says, "the first time in my life I could be free and open and myself." Although New York was no less welcoming in this sense, the social life he encountered was quite different and he missed the support network of his Parisian friends' group. "I actually spent a lot of time going back to Paris for the weekends," he remembers.

Finally, at the age of twenty-nine, after relentlessly working on his studies and career since his late teens, plus a year and a half in New York, in the summer of 2008, Thulstrup decided he needed to go home. He returned to Paris and spent a few weeks at a friend's country house just outside the city before deciding to go further "back home" to his parent's house in Copenhagen. As Catholics, his parents had not taken particularly well to his coming out at first and there had been some distance between them and their youngest son, but now they were nothing but supportive. He arrived home in time for his thirtieth birthday, and for the first time in his adult life, he took a break from work.

Thulstrup did not do much during this time except work on his portfolio a little. It was difficult for someone like him with so much drive and ambition to force himself to take things slowly. But after a while he started to reach out to his old styling contacts and find new jobs. "It was a tricky time because I had worked with Jean and Peter and did not see myself as a stylist anymore", he says. He had spent several years away from his home country working on some of the most prestigious interior design projects in the world. He knew that if he returned to accepting styling jobs again from his old Copenhagen clients, he would be shooting himself in the foot because people would be less likely to consider him for anything else. His options were either to find a job with another company or to do something that reflected what he felt he was capable of, so he established his own interior design practice. "Retrospectively, it was a wise decision," he says, "I turned down so many jobs. I think in my first year back home I only made 30,000 Krone. It was hard, but I knew I had to stay consistent and forge my own path."

Slowly, his interior architecture business started to pick up, at first with small jobs such as shop interiors and trade fair stands. On January 1, 2009, Thulstrup officially started his own company. For the first year, he worked alone from an office space in town that he shared with a graphic designer and a shoe designer. After that, he was able to rent his own work space and hire the first interns and employees, but he lived with his parents for a while longer. "They were very supportive," he says. "My siblings made fun of me a lot for it though. I had a great time living with my parents. I hadn't seen them for many years, and it had not gone down so well that I was gay, so to finally feel that they had opened their door to me to be home and be who I am was very special to me."

Flash forward fourteen years and Thulstrup is now an established interior architect with an international reputation. He has a thriving architecture business with a long string of highly prestigious interior architecture projects under his belt, including one of the world's best restaurants; a prestigious art park vineyard in Sonoma County; several private houses and apartments; and bars and cafes, as well as a significant number of retail outlets in China and Europe. He has not stinted when it comes to industrial design either and several of his furniture designs are in regular production.

When we spoke in his studio in late 2021, David Thulstrup had recently returned from a visit to his former childhood home with the new client who now owns it.

"I went up to see the house and, of course, it was completely destroyed. Its essence had been removed and dismantled. It was all painted white and light grey. The beautiful wood panelling was gone and the listed Greenlandic marble had been dug out and replaced. I have said 'yes' to the job because I need to bring soul back to this home. I needed to fix this place that is full of memories of my beginnings; the house in which who I am as a person and my creativity were founded."

And, as always, David Thulstrup set to work to do just that.

Georg Jensen
Munich, Germany

Georg Jensen, Munich

Tableau
Copenhagen, Denmark

 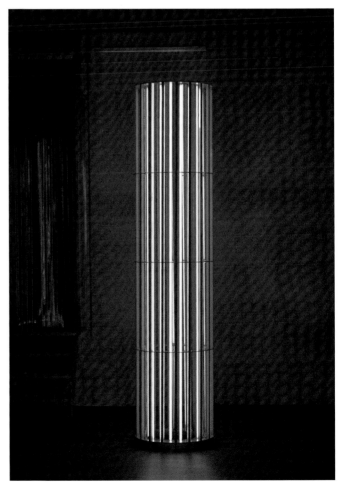

Blow
Copenhagen, Denmark

Georg Jensen
London, UK

Peter's House

Peter's House

Project: Residential and studio
Dimensions: 500 square metres (5,382 sq ft)
Location: Copenhagen, Denmark
Client: Peter Krasilnikoff
Completed: September 2015

Peter's House is Thulstrup's first complete residence where he both remodelled the entire structure and designed the interior. It was commissioned by photographer Peter Krasilnikoff, who asked Thulstrup to convert a former factory garage in Copenhagen's Islands Brygge harbour district into his private residence and studio while still maintaining its industrial feel.

The original garage building was a deep and dark space with three party walls and windows and doors that faced only to the front, so the biggest challenge was bringing light into the home. To resolve this issue, Thulstrup added an open-topped, glass- and mirror-walled atrium through the centre of the building. This combination not only pulled much-needed light into the interior, almost like a refracting chimney, but also created an optical effect, making the space seem far larger than it is.

An atrium, or *cavaedium*, is an ancient Roman invention, which brings a cool green space, an outdoor room, into the interior of a building. The garden in the atrium at the heart of Peter's house, measuring ten square metres (107 sq ft), has been planted in the manner of a natural Scandinavian woodland. In the centre sits a black alder tree, with ferns, moss, and wild anemones surrounding its base. When the sun shines, the reflected light passing through the green foliage casts dappled woodland-like shadows across the interior.

The new house has three floors. On the ground level, an open-plan kitchen, dining room and sitting room are arranged around the atrium. The floor is a raw, poured concrete screed, and the end-wall behind the kitchen is the original raw brick party wall – the rest of the exterior walls are a combination of concrete and blackened steel panelling. Around the atrium, the black-framed windows are offset by massive, oiled heart oak floorboards from the Danish flooring company Dinesen, which panel the remaining wall space.

These rather raw materials are offset by heavy floor-to-ceiling velvet Kvadrat curtains in dark navy and aubergine. Thulstrup designed several bespoke pieces of furniture for the house, including the dining table (also made from heart oak), a kitchen block clad in speckled terrazzo and a striking brass chandelier with exposed light bulbs that reflect in the windows and mirrors around the space when it is illuminated. The staircase – made of perforated one-centimetre-thick sheet steel (⅖ inch) – is also designed by Thulstrup. Its massive presence is lightened by its folded construction and the way the light from the atrium plays through the perforations.

Above the living area is the mezzanine floor where the primary bedroom and an ensuite bathroom and walk-in wardrobe are located. Here, the first floor's heavy concrete and dark curtains give way to wood on both the walls and floor and curtains in a pale peach-toned velvet. The terrazzo-lined bathroom is also a softer grey tone.

At the top of the house is a glass-walled roof-room, which Thulstrup designed as a study. This opens out onto an outdoor room that resembles a richly planted terrace landscape, complete with wood planters, seating areas, and an outdoor kitchen. The wood of the terrace is the same Brazilian hardwood that clads the entire building's facade in thin vertical strips. This extremely hard-wearing wood, Jatoba, or Brazilian cherry, weathers over time to a pale silvery grey, not unlike larch.

Peter's House

←←
The material mood board for Peter's House features purple velvet, natural heart oak, Italian terrazzo, blackened sheet steel for the kitchen and perforated blackened steel for the two staircases.

→
A view of one of the two bespoke staircases, that rise through the interior, seen here through the glass-walled landscaped atrium.

↓
The atrium, which is planted with a Black Alder tree as well as ferns, moss and wild anemones, is open to the sky, pulling light down three stories into the interior.

→→
The dining room, seen here through the mirrored atrium at night, features double-height purple velvet curtains and bespoke sculptural chandeliers.

→→→
The house, formerly a factory and garage, is clad with vertical slats of Brazilian hardwood that introduce a modulation of light and shade to both the interior and the exterior of the building.

Site plan

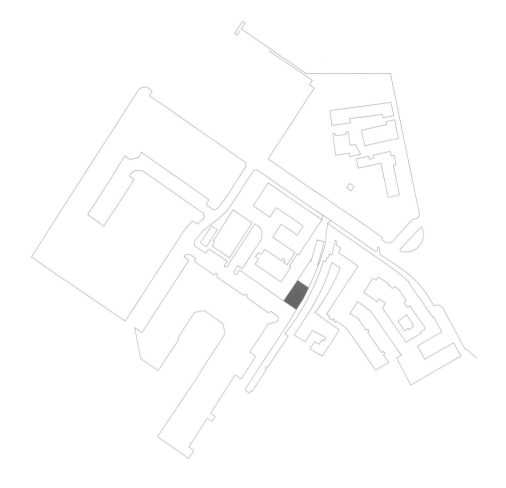

Elevation

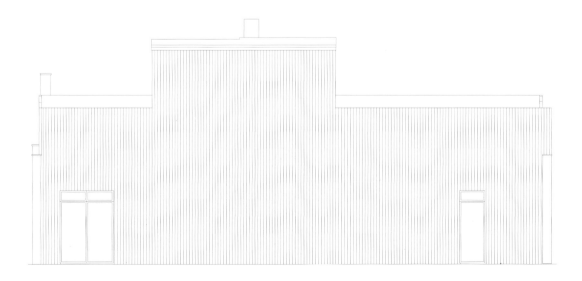

Peter's House

Peter's House

Second floor
plan

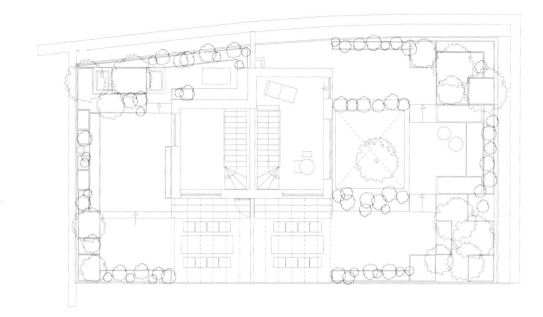

First floor
plan

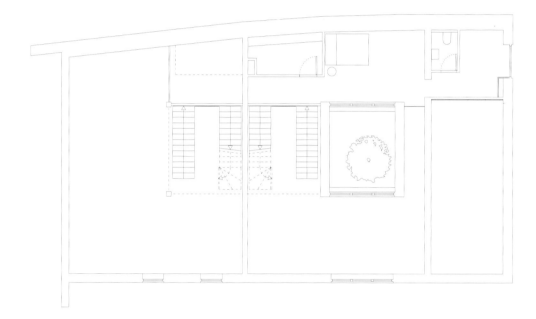

Ground floor
plan

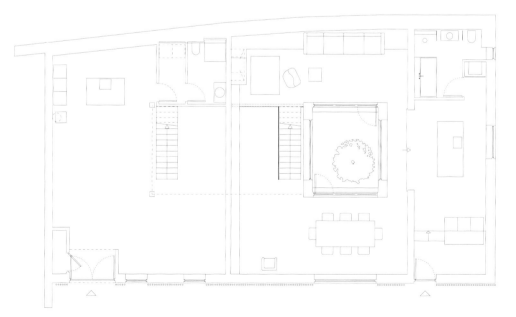

Peter's House

←←

The kitchen features a bespoke island counter and storage unit in terrazzo. The original brick wall has been stripped and cleaned and provides a textural contrast with the softness of the blue velvet curtains.

←

Blackened steel panelling in the kitchen clads the double-height wall.

→

Throughout the ground floor, raw poured concrete floors maintain the industrial quality of the original building and contrasts with the warm colours of the natural heart oak wall panelling.

↓

A view from underneath the stairs on the ground floor, across the landscaped atrium to the kitchen.

→→

The smoothness and precision of the bespoke terrazzo kitchen island is juxtaposed with the original raw brick wall, which itself becomes a textural backdrop for a collection of wooden masks and a selection of cooking tools.

Peter's House

Peter's House

←←
A view of the dining room wall where natural light from the atrium casts shadows that move across the various textures, materials and colours used in the interior, throughout the day.

←↑
The double-height dining room, which features a bespoke dining table and chandelier, is located directly adjacent to the atrium to maximize natural light.

→
A view from the dining room to the living room shows the interstitial space between the atrium and kitchen, with double height panels of blackened steel that contrast with the soft, pale pink curtains seen on the mezzanine above.

→→
In this view from the dining room into the kitchen, the natural oak boards that line the walls add a warmth, texture and colour that contrast with the blackened steel walls in the kitchen and the raw concrete floor.

Peter's House

← The bespoke staircases, which are welded together from sheets of ten-millimetre (⅓ inch) thick steel, are dematerialised by light from the atrium falling on their perforated surfaces.

↓ In the primary bedroom on the mezzanine level, natural heart oak boards cover the walls and floor, and pale textiles and brass accents lend an intimacy to the sleeping space.

→ A view from the living room to the dining room, where four of the key materials used throughout the interior can be experienced in concert – natural heart oak wall panels, floor-to-ceiling velvet curtains, perforated blackened steel and polished concrete.

Peter's House
Process

"Peter's House was my first large architectural construction project and while it came with various challenges and complexities, it was also an invaluable learning experience. The level of complexity that came with constructing a whole new building inside the carefully demolished remnants of another – brought with it some significant challenges.

The site was an industrial garage with very old brick walls and dilapidated wooden cladding. From the beginning I knew that a huge amount of work would need to be done, both to rectify any of the structure we wanted to keep, and to build what is essentially a completely new three bedroom house and separate photographic studio.

We ended up knocking down all the columns as well as the street facade, keeping only three external brick walls, and one internal wall. Following the demolition, a concrete floor was poured and an entirely new steel framework was inserted into the stripped out building. The brick walls were then pressure cleaned, and finally the entire site was stripped and emptied ready for the timber framing for the internal walls and intermediate floors to be built up off the load-bearing concrete floor and new steel and timber structure.

One of the challenges, but also a very satisfying aspect of the finished

design, was the use of blackened steel for one of the new walls, as well as a perforated version of the same steel for the stair.

It was tricky to find the right combination of structural stability, versus both the actual and the visual weight of the material. I worked closely with the engineer and the manufacturer of the stair to resolve the complexity of aesthetic lightness and structural integrity. The day the stair was delivered to site and craned into position was really special. It was both very tense, and very exciting, waiting to see if it would fit. It was a huge relief when it all came together on site and had just the right depth, strength and transparency we had imagined.

It was a similar experience with the trees. Seeing a crane bring six-metre-tall (20 foot) trees into the atrium was both stressful and exciting. Elsewhere in the landscaping installation, we had a significant challenge in that the massive planters on the roof terraces were not going to be strong enough to support the weight of the earth that needed to go into them. To resolve this, we urgently had to re-do the calculations and reinforce all the seating that surrounds the planters.

I am incredibly happy with the result, as is the client. Together we embraced every challenge and are very proud of the finished product."

A Sense of Place
Stedsans

"Whenever you enter a new place, you know within seconds whether or not you like being there; you know instantly whether it is good or bad."

A human being's sensitivity to atmosphere is the result of a complex set of intangibles that are often hard to articulate, and yet we can feel them with extraordinary precision. Atmospheres evoke feelings that range from the sense of individual insignificance in the face of an alpine vista to the comforting warmth and protection of a fire in a domestic hearth. Upon entering an environment, we sense that place with all our faculties: the smells, the temperature and humidity, the light, the movement of air, the tactility of the materials, the colour palette and the acoustics. Within a split second, we can subconsciously calculate whether the atmosphere of a place is safe and welcoming or potentially hostile – one in which we can relax our guard or need to raise it – regardless of whether it is new and intriguing or familiar and comforting.

In the late 1950s, the American abstract painter Mark Rothko was commissioned to create a series of paintings for the Four Seasons restaurant in New York's Seagram Building, designed by the architect Mies van der Rohe. Rothko was known for his large canvases with vibrant planes of colour built-up from many layers of transparent glazes; his paintings hum with mood-altering atmospheres that were created through fields of colour. For this commission – an interior space designed by another architect, Philip Johnson – Rothko chose a colour palette of deep maroons, wine reds, greys and blacks for seven huge canvases to fit the proportions of the space. But Rothko's aim was reportedly far from wanting to create a convivial atmosphere for diners; rather, it was a dramatic act of colour-field sabotage. In his dislike of the high-end restaurant (which he only visited after he accepted the commission), he was subconsciously influenced, he later said, by Michelangelo's oppressive, windowless staircase room for the Laurentian Library in Florence. Michelangelo, Rothko said, "achieved just the kind of feeling I'm after – he makes the viewers feel that they are trapped in a room where all the doors and windows are bricked up so that all they can do is butt their heads forever against the wall."[1]

Ultimately, Rothko withdrew from the commission rather than hang his paintings in a space he disliked so much. A decade later, he donated nine paintings from the series to the Tate Gallery in London, which had offered to create a room to house them according to very specific instructions from Rothko with respect to lighting, wall colour and hanging. The resulting windowless Rothko Room is a powerful example of the sublime effect an atmosphere created primarily through colour fields can have, with proportion and light playing supportive roles. The room's atmosphere almost grabs the viewer and forces them into subdued contemplation; such is the potential power of interior architecture.

As an interior architect, David Thulstrup's job is all about creating atmospheres. Like Rothko, he manipulates intangibles through the use of tangibles in order to generate environments for the senses. This skill comes through knowing how to work with scale, sizes, volumes and materials in order to influence emotions. Yet, unlike the example of the recalcitrant Rothko above, Thulstrup creates spaces that people want to be in, spaces with good atmospheres that are welcoming. "This can be achieved in so many ways", he says, "but often it works best when the individual can resonate with the space – when it feels comfortable because it is semi-familiar."

Around 2011, when his own practice was still in relative infancy, Thulstrup began to work with the huge fashion retail group Bestseller Fashion Group China, which owns several brands operating out of some seven thousand outlets across five hundred cities in China. Founded by three Danish entrepreneurs – Anders Holch Povelsen, Dan Friis and Allan Warburg – Bestseller is always on the lookout for young, fresh design talent, and the three executives were drawn to the welcoming, "simple style" of Thulstrup's designs. So they flew him out for an initial meeting, and not long after, offered him a commission that would shape the next stage of his business.

Bestseller entrusted Thulstrup with the development of concepts for three of their brands, and for the next eight years, he would go on to create one to two completely new retail designs for them each year, which would then be rolled out in several hundred stores throughout China. "He was very hungry, very interested in the project," says Allan Warburg of one of the reasons for giving such a huge commission to the young designer. "We felt he was going to give it everything and he really did."

Once Thulstrup's retail concept for one of the brands had been agreed on with the client, a full-scale mock-up of the design was built within one of the brand's factory spaces, allowing its own team to evaluate the viability of the design and the quality of the materials. "I learned so much from working with them," says Thulstrup. "The process of working with a professional client that has the capacity to support like that is incredible."

Creating an interior concept at this level and applying it across several hundred stores involves a lot of logistics and an interesting take on recycling.

"At two-year intervals, we would do designs for around four A-class stores, and then they would evaluate and implement the designs into a series of four hundred A-class stores in the top-tier cities such as Beijing, Shanghai and Shenzhen. In parallel to refurbishing these existing stores, the old 'new' fixtures and fittings would be reinstalled in, say, eight hundred B-location stores, and the former interiors from them, the old, old 'new,' would be reinstalled in perhaps twelve hundred C-location stores. So there is a rolling recycling chain there of sorts."

Thulstrup says that those years of working on the rollercoaster of large-scale fashion retail design – learning to invent and create new atmospheres to titillate the sensorium of the buying public – gave him a phenomenal amount of experience at many levels. He and his team of, by then, fourteen staff, kept pace with global style developments and trends at all times, but they also acquired a deep understanding of how consumers operate within an environment.

"There are so many aspects you need to consider in retail: the digital aspect, storage, functionality within the space; how people navigate it and what attracts their attention When you work with a client that large, with that amount of experience, they also have a tremendous amount of knowledge of their own to bring to the table."

What Thulstrup learned from Bestseller during that process he can now bring to all of his retail projects, particularly about how to use design decisions to affect sales, where to place product categories and, perhaps more importantly, when to turn standard retail conventions on their head.

This experience with Bestseller also garnered him more recognition, and Thulstrup began to get commissions for high-end European brands. In 2015 he designed retail interiors for the Danish luxury silversmiths Georg Jensen in both Munich and London (see pages 18 and 26). Because of his work with Bestseller, Thulstrup was now able to apply all his knowledge about the organisation, process and workflow that is needed to create both a retail experience and technological expressions.

"With the high street brands in China, we got to test out a lot of new digital technologies. For example, service technology for fitting rooms, or mobile devices for customers to pay on the shop floor, which was not possible ten years ago. Much of this could be implemented in luxury environments as well."

The difference with a heritage brand like Georg Jensen, in terms of generating a special atmosphere, is that the designer has an entire historical layer already in place to work with. There's an existing storyline. In high-street retail, the storylines often need to be invented from scratch by the designer as well. There are also big differences in product density, which can affect how the designer treats the space.

"In a high-end store, there is lower density, which means the customer can pay attention to the atmosphere and tactility of the space because they are more exposed to it. In a high-street outlet, however, the products are often stacked so high and close together that you don't really see what's behind them. These are things that you have to be very aware of when creating concepts."

With the Georg Jensen commissions, other high-end jobs started to roll into Thulstrup's studio from retail to hospitality and residential sectors. With these projects, Thulstrup took his love of creating a sense of place to a contextual level that had always appealed to him. Reminiscent of the way his first childhood home was so strongly bound to its location and its history, a pattern began to emerge in which Thulstrup increasingly used historical, geographical and chronological tools in new and unexpected ways to tie sensory impressions to the spaces he created.

The interior design of the Aarhus women's store (see page 154) for the Danish multi-brand fashion and accessories brand Collage from 2018 is a good example of how Thulstrup gives context through a form of historical storytelling. Located in a former pharmacy in the city's old town centre, the building features a decoratively painted stucco ceiling dating from 1929. Thulstrup's own style, reflected in the design he created for the shop, is one of clean lines and monolithic textured planes. The conventional retail design path would have been to cover up the ceiling along with the rest of the historical interior in order to transplant this completely new vision into the space. Instead, Thulstrup chose to incorporate the original ceiling – from a completely different era – into his Collage interior, ultimately making the ongoing story of the building and its location visible – a collage of time. "You can tell the story of a building that has been there for many years by making sure it

is not forgotten, perhaps by letting elements stay and not covering them up. Or you can tell stories of what used to be there but isn't any more by bringing elements back in the form of materials," he explains. "When I start a project, I always try to dive into its history, its story: What was on the site? What was in the building? And then I make sure this remains present in some way – not in an exaggerated, comical fashion, but in a small or understated element. I always want to find that narrative that gives things a meaning or purpose."

So he kept the ceiling visible and inserted his new interior below it, separating the two – past and present – with a "force field" of long, narrow, parallel tracks of LED lights, which are not only a brand-defining feature he created for all his Collage store designs, but in this instance created an interesting atmosphere, like that of being at a fold in the fabric of time where two eras can almost touch one another. The historical ceiling is there, and at the same time, it was there and will be there, just as the present contains a mixture of the past and future. It is a poetic juxtaposition, and at the same time, a highly atmospheric way of creating a sense of place as a nexus in time.

When Thulstrup is designing, he opens dialogues. Perhaps the most important of those dialogues is the one between himself and the places he is given to work with. As a result, there is a naturalness to the spaces he creates. His designs do not need to fight for recognition because they appear to belong and reflect the continuity of that place in time; they are part of the *terroir*. "Respecting what's there, what you put in and the limitations of a space are important," he says. "I try not to force anything onto a space."

In these dialogues with the local environment, Thulstrup places particular emphasis on materials to generate a sense of place through his designs.

"It starts outside, outside with nature. I focus on the colours of flowers, stones and earth, or contrasts in something like a fallen tree trunk. In cityscapes, I always keep visual diaries on my phone of compositions and materials that are almost like little guidebooks made up of zoomed images of materials and surfaces. Everywhere I go, I focus on the *stedsans* (pronounced *stillsense*), this 'sense of place' through the existing material palette. Diving into a material palette of a city or place is very important to me and very inspiring."

Henry David Thoreau said, in *Walden*; or, *Life in the Woods* (1854): "Live in each season as it passes; breathe the air, drink the drink, taste the fruit, and resign yourself to the influence of the earth." The absolute classic – and now world-famous – example in Thulstrup's work where the sense of place reflects a perfectly designed confluence of place, people and purpose is his 2018 interior design for Noma, a three-Michelin-starred restaurant in Copenhagen (see page 77). The restaurant, its kitchens, greenhouses, storerooms and reception rooms are housed in an interconnecting, free-standing cluster of single-storey buildings, a former navy arsenal designed and repurposed by BIG architects, nestled beside a small woodland and a garden designed by Piet Oudolf by the Christianshavn waterfront.

Thulstrup's interior for Noma is created from elemental materials of the finest quality that have been worked by highly skilled craftspeople. Each guest enters the space on a terrazzo of river stones, worn smooth over time, which gives way to two-hundred-year-old oak floorboards in the dining rooms. Functional greenhouses filled with herbs and plants destined for the table are followed by a reception space with walls of heart oak planks. The surfaces of the dining room walls are the exposed end grain of stacks of massive oak planks. There are occasional tables made from solid blocks of Swedish granite, and others made from ancient oak timbers salvaged from the harbour's waters and from the days when it would have taken an entire forest of oaks to build a single ship. Thulstrup also designed the dining tables and chairs, which were custom-made by Danish master joiners Brdr. Krüger.

Thulstrup's design for Noma is a sublime interpretation of *terroir* – of a sense of place. It is a homely one that speaks to the soul that, like Henry David Thoreau, longs for a simple cabin in the woods by the side of a lake. Yet at the same time, in providing a seamless setting for the highly seasonal and exceptional cuisine of the "Best Restaurant in the World",[2] it is extraordinary in the luxury of its materiality and craftsmanship.

René Redzepi, chef and co-owner of Noma, worked closely with Thulstrup in the creation of this sense of place for his restaurant – something that is more domestic than dramatic, more homestead than haute cuisine:

> "The interior architecture translates from how we cook. Everything we do is about translating a season onto a plate, and the plates themselves are made from the soil that the very ingredients come from. Everything is a dish. Everything is a plate of food. The materials for the interior are from the same woods that the mushrooms come from. The stone could be quarried 100 kilometres (62 miles) from where the seafood lands every morning. To have that feeling of connection to the land also creates a feeling of well-being. like being in a beautiful forest on a sunny day or having a view of a mountainside. For me, the best interiors have this connection, and I think David pretty much nailed it at Noma. It does not feel disconnected from nature; it feels like it's a part of it."

For the Romantics, the sublime occurs when our rational selves are overridden by emotions sparked by an awe of the natural world. If you are an Edmund Burke fan, the sublime can be terrifying because it draws attention to our insignificance. The sublime aspect of the Noma interior is a more convivial one arising from a subtle combination of the generous use of very precious and ancient natural materials (a direct reflection of the preciousness of the natural ingredients of the restaurant's cuisine) that have been treated with reverence and fine craftsmanship. The elements of the interior clearly have the potential to far outlive the lives of both the guests and the builders. They are imbued with the ancient and the new all at once. Again, Thulstrup has generated here a nexus of time, that slowed moment in the neck of the hourglass anchoring the visitor into the familiar comfort and safe material solidity of the place, yet still keeping them aware of the vast flow of time in which they are but riding on a tiny grain. Redzepi says:

> "It's a design that requires deep attention. There is so much quality, so much attention to detail that if you allow yourself to look for them, you'll be swimming in them for days. Some people might say it's simple or that it reminds them of something, but there are many, many parts of [the interior] that are incredibly ground-breaking and fresh and different. We didn't go for a place that was very homely at all. We wanted to push the boundaries, but in a different way."

This sense of place at Noma created through materials and handcraft, as well as attention to the needs of the user, also has historical parallels in the roots of Danish design tradition. Historically, Danish modernism has tended to embrace a warmer and more pragmatic functional approach through its use of natural and regional materials than its central European counterparts. "Denmark was industrialised rather late at the end of the nineteenth century, though fully implemented only after World War II. It was a traditional farmer nation with an outstanding craft tradition," says Anne-Louise Sommer, director of the Designmuseum Denmark. Whereas many Western countries fully embraced mass production and modern materials after World War II, Denmark was one of the few that continued to preserve fine craftsmanship, especially within the furniture industry. Its design education at the time also continued to prioritise craft and furniture making in parallel to welcoming the functionalist principles of modernism. "To become an architect or designer in the twentieth century you had to have a practical craft education before you started at the school of architecture or design," adds Sommer. "So all the great Danish masters – Arne Jacobsen, Hans J. Wegner,

Børge Mogensen, Poul Kjærholm – all of them were craftsmen before they became trained architects and designers."

The northern Danish climate means long, dark winters during which, for most people, the majority of their time is spent indoors. The Danes, like other Nordic nations, have long been experts in countering the inhospitable winter climate with the hospitable atmospheres of their interiors. They even have a special word to describe such atmospheres: *hygge*. "The home has always meant a lot to the Danes, which also explains why they have been willing to invest a lot of money in high-quality design products that last for a long time," explains Sommer.

> "David's design can be seen as a new interpretation of this Danish design tradition with an emphasis on natural materials, traditional furniture types and simple, minimalistic forms. There is a strong resonance in his work when it comes to the quintessential 'Danishness'. High-quality, long-lasting products suitable for different purposes – with an international touch as well. An intelligent reinterpretation of the heritage. David's care for the human whole in his spaces is also very typically Danish. For me, it expresses a humanistic, user-centred approach which is one of the most important aspects when it comes to good design."

A sense of place is always relative, and a sense of identity through place even more so. In a globalised world, the idea of nationality-specific attributes is a knotty subject. What is Danishness in the twenty-first century? Thulstrup trained in the contextual and very international world of Jean Nouvel's practice in Paris, as well as the equally international, luxurious materiality of high-end fashion with Peter Marino's studio. Like his fellow Danish architect and designer Bodil Kjær, who trained with Finn Juhl and studied in Copenhagen a generation before, Thulstrup's international work experience and sensibility are clearly evident in his work.

"Personally, I'm not too keen on trendy categorisations," says Farah Ebrahimi, the art director and partner of Philipp Mainzer, founder of the German furniture brand e15.

> "Perhaps it's easier for the press to encapsulate a look or style with a catchy term, but it's not so helpful in extending a larger conversation on design, society, culture or the work of a designer. I think David is very perceptive and gifted, he draws inspiration from his experiences, travels, and of course his Scandinavian roots in the way he utilises light, form, material and colour. His work doesn't just belong to Northern Europe, his taste and aesthetic is worldly."

"Maybe Danish Design is more of a brand than a style today," suggests Anne-Louise Sommer, meaning that labels that get attached to furniture and utensils in the commercial world have more to do with selling than production. It is certainly true that an appreciation for fine craftsmanship, a penchant for warm simplicity and reverence for materials could just as easily be attributed to Japanese design heritage, or that of religious groups, such as the Shakers, or any one of a number of cultural maker traditions. Maker aesthetics and techniques are to a large extent born out of humble necessity, climate or material restrictions as well as religious and cultural mores. They are both part of the human condition and a reflection of the very best of human ingenuity. We are toolmakers and place makers, good ones at that. Danish or not, David Thulstrup is a master place maker in this respect.

1 Quoted in: Christopher Rothko, *Mark Rothko: From the Inside Out* (Yale University Press, New Haven and London, 2015), p.133

2 *Restaurant* magazine awarded the accolade in 2010, 2011, 2012 and 2014, in addition to the World's 50 Best Restaurants Award in 2021.

Les Nouvelles Galeries
Annecy, France

Garde Hvalsøe
Aarhus, Denmark

Gasoline
Copenhagen, Denmark

Otto
Copenhagen, Denmark

Noma

Noma

Project: Restaurant
Dimensions: 1,200 square metres (12,916 sq ft)
Location: Copenhagen, Denmark
Client: Noma
Completed: February 2018

For David Thulstrup, being asked to design the interiors for the new home of Noma, one of the world's best and most famous restaurants, was a very special commission. The site comprises eleven individual buildings that are grouped around a former arsenal located near Freetown Christiania. For the client, chef René Redzepi, the most important consideration was for the restaurant interior to feel like home. "Our team is living in this space for the majority of our lives, so we have to feel at home." It also needed to be a space that "feels modern but handmade" with "materials that come from craft and tradition."

To achieve this homely feeling at Noma, Thulstrup specifically aimed to create a residential rather than a hospitality design. He counteracted the higher wear and tear that a restaurant interior is subjected to with very high-quality and hard-wearing natural materials, such as oak and stone, and excellent craftsmanship. In principle at least, a well-crafted, bespoke interior made of strong, honest and durable materials can withstand the stresses of use over decades, if not centuries.

The atmosphere in the main hospitality rooms is contemporary yet timeless. Comprising a cluster of buildings with huge windows that look out onto the Piet Oudolf-designed garden and the broad waters of Erdkehlgraven, the restaurant feels rural yet without pastiche. The original design came quickly to Thulstrup, but it took more than a year to select the materials and surface treatments and complete the interiors. He also had to design all of the cabinetry, tables, chairs, sofas and lighting, as well as select complementary artworks.

Guests enter the restaurant through a string of greenhouses that run through the garden, full of culinary plants used by the kitchen. The restaurant building entrance is framed with walls of solid heart oak, which contrast with a sandblasted terrazzo floor of rounded river stones that flows through all the circulation areas. This cedes into a floor of huge butterfly-jointed heart oak in the main dining area, douglas fir in the private dining area, and a handmade brick floor in the lounge. Between the guest areas is a service kitchen island – much like an open home kitchen – also custom-built from oak. The area between the entrance, lounge and dining rooms is panelled with natural oak throughout.

The walls of the main dining room, which seats forty-two, are lined with stacked oak planks that are held together by 250,000 concealed screws. Large picture windows afford views onto the garden and the harbour beyond. The Arv round tables and Arv dining chairs, with seats and backs of woven paper cord, were designed by Thulstrup and made by Brdr. Krüger, a traditional family-run Danish furniture maker, now in its fifth generation. The lighting was designed in collaboration with the Austrian firm XAL and Thulstrup commissioned young Danish designer Jonas Edvard to create the custom conical light shades using locally sourced gesso. A stack of huge blackened two-hundred-year-old timber beams that were dredged out of the nearby harbour acts as a counter in the centre of the room, which is otherwise deliberately unadorned to allow Noma's in-house stylist Christine Rudolph to work her seasonal magic with displays of found and foraged natural materials.

The private dining room is a more intimate space, which looks out onto a leafy little woodland area. The room's centrepiece is a six-metre-long (19 foot) table, also made by Brdr. Krüger, which was crafted from three planks of a 160-year-old tree from the island of Fyn. The entire room is made of white oiled Douglas fir including the built-in shelving. The bespoke credenza was created by cabinetmaker Malte Gormsen, and the custom-made seaweed lampshades by designer Jonas Edvard. The built-in shelves on one wall accommodate an archive of Noma artefacts including objects from their pop-ups in Australia and Mexico. The wall lamps, like the rest of the furnishings, are also Thulstrup's designs.

At the end of their meal, guests move into the airy lounge, which, again, affords views across the garden and lake through large oak-framed windows. The space's walls and floor are a custom-made brickwork by Petersen Tegl, complete with an integrated open fireplace and a wood ceiling. The pale leather two- and three-seater sofas are also custom Thulstrup designs, as are the massive dark Swedish granite coffee tables, featuring smooth tops and rough-hewn edges. The Finnish lounge chairs by Nikari are upholstered in either natural leather or linen, and the room's blue cushions were made by a Faroese weaver. Lighting is a combination of pendant lights and vintage lampshades by Jørgen Wolff, with ceiling spotlights designed together with XAL. Noma is an ongoing project that is constantly in the process of being refined.

In 2021, Thulstrup was asked to extend the hospitality experience into the row of greenhouses in the garden, which are used to grow produce for the restaurant. The greenhouses lead from the entrance to the property and guests pass through them on the way in. Under a metal and hemp shade, which screens the sun from above, there is now a lounge area filled with more custom-made pine furniture, natural-coloured thick wool Kvadrat cushions and curtain dividers made from potato-sack fabric. Surrounded by the luxuriant growth of carefully tended culinary plants, this has become a place for guests to leave the day behind and relax before continuing their culinary journey.

←←
The material mood board for the entrance and kitchen space features a bespoke terrazzo floor of river-stones, two-hundred-year-old pine reclaimed from the Copenhagen harbour, oak wood and brass alloy panels.

→
The material mood board for the lounge area includes custom-made light bricks, Swedish granite and natural wool carpets.

↓
The material mood board for the main dining room comprises different kinds of treated oak, natural heart oak, smoked oak, white oiled oak as well as two-hundred-year-old reclaimed pine.

↘
The material mood board for the private dining room includes douglas pine wood, two-hundred-year-old reclaimed pine and locally sourced seaweed.

Site plan

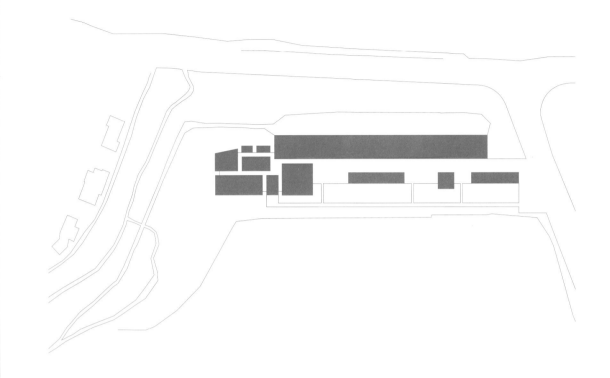

Floor plan

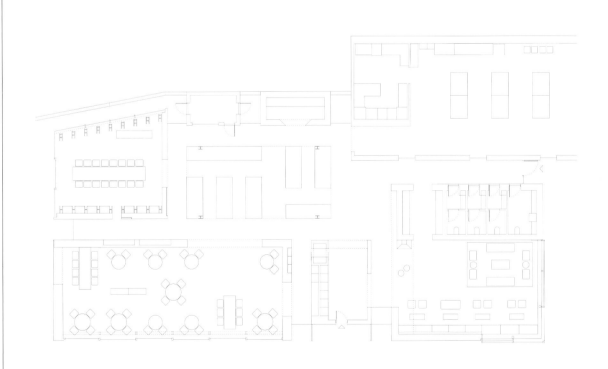

Noma

←←
Guests enter through a greenhouse where they are seated on Karm sofas designed by David Thulstrup, to enjoy a welcome drink. Natural materials including brick, hemp textile and pine, combined with plants and a fireplace, create a warm and inviting atmosphere.

←
In the entrance space a bespoke terrazzo floor of locally sourced river stones is juxtaposed with walls of solid oak planks and brass alloy panels.

↓
The entrance is lit by a glass roof, bringing in an abundance of natural light and revealing the quality, colour and texture of the materials including brick, and wood as well as the roughness of the firewood stacked for use in the kitchen.

→
Elsewhere in the entrance space, a wall-hung artwork by Carl Emil Jacobsen made from crushed stone and gypsum sits in contrast to a seasonal table display of preserving jars containing different species of octopus.

←
Once inside the main entrance space guests can admire the ceiling-hung artwork titled *Conscious Compass* by Olafur Eliasson commissioned specially for Noma and made from driftwood and raw earth magnets.

→
In the entry space a wall of bricks brings a colour range from dark burnt ochre to a creamy white, complementing the monochromatic palette elsewhere in the design.

↓
Natural oak panels line the ceiling and walls of the entrance space, some of them concealing integrated coat cupboards.

←

In the main dining area, monolithic slabs of reclaimed timber have been used as a serving table and a vertical sculpture. Here, the ceiling is lined in oak battens, and the walls have been clad with thousands of stacked planks of end-grain oak wood.

→

In the main dining space, the Arv chairs, which were designed by David Thulstrup specially for Noma, are made from oak and paper cord. Complementing them are the circular Arv tables in oak as well as custom made tables made from old, reclaimed pine that lend a quality of aged endurance and strength to the interior.

↓

For each of Noma's three seasons, which they refer to as "sea", "summer" and "game", the decorations shift to reflect the changing time of year. The dining room is shown here in "sea" season with seaweed adorning some of the natural oak beams.

←
A view of the private dining room, built entirely from Douglas Pine, where locally sourced seaweed lamp shades in a range of natural colours are changed for each of Noma's three seasons.

↑
The waiter's station in the private dining room is made from two-hundred-year-old pine reclaimed from Copenhagen Harbour.

→ →→
Throughout the restaurant the contemporary sophistication and refined finish of the Arv chairs by David Thulstrup are used in contrast to custom designed, monolithic tables in old, reclaimed pine.

Noma

Noma

←←
A view of the lounge area in the evening. Here, the walls and floor are made from custom-made creamy white bricks, and low tables in solid blocks of black granite.

←
The fireplace is constructed from creamy white custom-made bricks and features a vintage mid-century cast iron firedog by artist Olle Hermansson.

↑
The picture windows in the lounge are framed in natural heart oak and feature a built-in bench with natural leather upholstery.

↗
The lounge features a specially commissioned yellow pigment concrete plinth by artists Pettersen & Hein.

→
The lounge bar features a monolithic oak tabletop supported on a block of black Swedish granite in the lounge bar.

→→
The custom-made coffee tables in black Swedish granite with smooth top and rough sides contrasts with the custom floor rug, and David Thulstrup's Karm Sofa, both in pale grey natural wool.

Noma

Noma
Process

"When I was commissioned to design the interior and furniture for the new Noma restaurant, just one of the buildings (of eleven that would make up the final complex) existed. My first challenge was to understand and decipher the intentions of the architect, Bjarke Ingels Group (BIG) who were already on board, and create a palette of materials that was in agreement with BIG's intentions for the architecture. The overlap between the architect's work, and mine was complex to negotiate because there is no discernible point at which the outside and the inside of a building start or finish. As a result, I undertook a lot of detailed coordination with BIG to get the architecture and the interior to work seamlessly together.

The biggest challenge however, was the limited time period – I had just fourteen months from breaking ground to completion. Due to the compressed schedule, many decisions had to be made on site. With so many different specialist trades on site at the same time, it was like designing eight separate projects at once. The dining room, entrance foyer, lounge, dining, and kitchen – each of the key spaces needed to be constructed and finished simultaneously. The sequencing of trades that would usually ensure the safe progression of the building work was not possible, so we often had brick

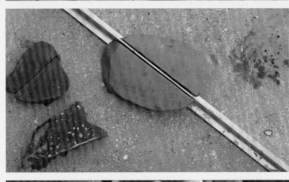

layers, carpenters, and other tradespeople on site at the same time.

One of the most unique aspects was the terrazzo floor made from stones sourced from Danish rivers. I put together a range of samples showing how different sized, shaped and coloured stones could be grouped together, so that the terrazzo contractor could match my intention. Like all the materials I specified, the stones make a direct reference to nature in the wild, but at Noma have been used to create a beautiful and comfortable space to spend time. René loved the terrazzo – he was very much taken with the image of people taking their shoes off and feeling like they were walking on a riverbed.

The reclaimed pine was another extraordinary material I had an opportunity to work with at Noma. On a visit to the warehouse of the cabinet maker who was making all the joinery for the project, he mentioned, almost in passing, that he had a cache of massive chunks of reclaimed wood that happened to have been dredged up more than fifteen years previously, from the river right in front of what eventually became the site for the new Noma. The pine had been driven into the riverbed as piles hundreds of years ago as part of the local shipbuilding industry. I immediately saw the potential for these

beautiful and rare artefacts to take pride of place at Noma. Some of them were just the right size to be used as table legs, while others were placed in-situ just as they were, as sculptural elements.

The greatest lesson I learned at Noma was the power of optimism and teamwork. It was a huge challenge to put together so many bespoke elements that needed to be designed from scratch – from fireplaces, to furniture, to lights as well as special finishes for all of the walls, floors, ceilings and joinery.

It usually takes three years to design a single chair and get it into production – here I had to do it all in just eight months. But the way everyone pulled together to make it happen was extraordinary. Noma was, without a doubt, one of the most complex projects I have ever undertaken, but ultimately a hugely rewarding one."

Massive Materiality
Væsentlighed

"I take the stone. I take the rock. I take it inside."

In the late twentieth and early twenty-first centuries, Danish households were not the only ones to be seduced by the low cost and availability of mass-produced "design" furniture. From the early 1970s, the Scandinavian design aesthetic of white walls, blonde wood and furniture made from composite materials gained increasing dominance throughout homes across the globe. It is an aesthetic that David Thulstrup struggles with. "White minimalism is, for me, not Danish," he says. "It is a misunderstanding of simplicity." Simplicity for him lies in the tradition of handcraft, minimalistic forms, and even warm planes of colour. Most of all, simplicity, for Thulstrup, goes hand-in-hand with the use of individual, predominantly natural materials. His design is built upon his relationship with, and approach to, materials and the materiality of his interiors – brick, steel, stone, wood and leather – are materials he sees as being essential, pure, honest and eternal.

When Thulstrup recalls his childhood home, it is the materials he mentions first: the Greenlandic marble floors, dark wood panelling, exposed wooden beams and decorative plasterwork. For him, it is materiality combined with volume that give a place soul. He believes that the richness and luxury of high-quality materials have been forgotten in Danish (and Scandinavian) design, and he intends to bring them back with his work.

"Massive materiality" is one of Thulstrup's favourite expressions when explaining his goals for, and appreciation of, a space or surface. It is an interesting exercise to attempt to understand what he means by it. He is not referring to the huge and complex, synthetic, multi-component-built layers of "stuff" defining our Anthropocene age. In fact, it is quite the opposite. He uses the term to describe the atmosphere or emotional effect generated by using a mono-material mass or surface within a space. A coffee table made from a solitary block of hewn granite, for example, a dining table made from the single trunk of a two-hundred-year-old tree, or a wall of handmade bricks; massive, as in "mass", but not monumental. "I am a strong believer in the tactility of materials, and I often create through that," he

explains. "Sometimes it's about the gesture, like a very strong, single-material element. Sometimes it's about how different materials meld together and create something that correlates."

This approach is one that corresponds with that of the premium furniture brand e15, which has collaborated with Thulstrup on some of his furniture projects. "Very much like David, we believe in mono-materiality as it plays a strong role at the core of beautiful and compelling spaces," says Farah Ebrahimi, art director and partner at e15. In 2019, Ebrahimi and her partner Philipp Mainzer, co-founder of the company, visited Thulstrup in his studio to discuss the production of custom bar stools for an interior project he was working on, and they discovered they had this common interest. "He's very good at creating environments that are composed without being too tricky or pushed to look a certain way. There are certain elements that harmonise in their materiality and function to form these environments. David's spaces don't appear staged or inflexible, in effect they inspire and allow for individual expression", she adds.

The environment she is specifically referring to here is Gasoline (see page 72), a restaurant in Copenhagen that Thulstrup designed in 2019. The key material element of this space is galvanized steel for both the open kitchen and the long diner counter. The metal surfaces are softened with the juxtaposition of a warm, pale fawn textured terrazzo for the countertop and flooring. A third material in the space is the solid European oak of Thulstrup's custom-designed bar stools lined up at the counter. It was these "Tank" bar stools that Thulstrup initially asked e15 to custom-make for the restaurant, and they liked them so much that they put them into production as part of the e15 portfolio.

One of the most precious tools of Thulstrup's trade is his extensive materials archive. It is meticulously organised and catalogued, and takes up a fair portion of his studio space. The archive currently comprises some twelve tonnes (thirteen US tons) of materials as well as spots, lamps, taps, rails, handles, knobs, hooks and other fixtures and fittings. This private library of interior ingredients is displayed on over one hundred metres (328 ft) of shelving in eight massive units. "I felt completely at home in David's studio," affirms Ebrahimi. "He's got loads of materials and samples that are so well organised. It's like being in a room full of treasure."

Despite always striving for simplicity in his work, there is a part of Thulstrup that is an avid collector and his archive is the place where he can allow himself to indulge that. His attraction to materials is as much haptic as it is visual so putting together material mood boards is a large part of his creative process.

> "I love having materials to hand. I need to see and feel them as I work. When we research a project that specifies metal mesh, for example, we might end up with fifty different sheet samples. We send back what we know we are never going to work with, and the ones we like are added to the archive. So slowly, over time, I have ended up with a massive collection of materials I really love."

Thulstrup uses his archive like a well-stocked larder from which he can draw ingredients at a moment's notice. "When I have clients coming into the studio, I can sit them down at the table and bring selected materials to them," he says. "It's like a questionnaire. It helps me understand where they are coming from, and it's a very important way of starting to engage in a dialogue – a dialogue between myself, the client, the materials and the space."

The masses or quantities of matter Thulstrup refers to in his material choices tend to be dense. Oak, one of his favourite woods, is an incredibly strong, close-grained and durable hardwood. Granite is the definition of massive in rock form – dense, heavy and extremely hard. Stainless steel is right up there in the heavy (meaning durable) metal department. His preferences tend towards the use of natural materials as much for environmental reasons as for "honesty" and durability. He

tends to prefer natural stone and wood as well as materials that are local to the region but he is not precious about it:

> "I don't mind synthetics sometimes, but they tend to come in as small gestures. It's not so much about the amount of material either as the way that I apply it. I often make rooms based on creating architectural sculptures or volumes within. These mono-material volumes have a massive material element to them as well – within more calm surroundings."

He uses his material volumes in a very primal way, like protagonists, blocking space – as in defining the action – within interiors as if they were a theatre stage or film set. Occasionally a single material and form can take a starring role and become the main protagonist of one of Thulstrup's interiors, such as the glass-blasted steel spiral staircase in the main living space of his 2020 residential project Vester Voldgade (see page 167), with its yellow-electroplated zinc finish that has iridescent dashes of green, pink and blue.

At other times, Thulstrup works with materiality all over the space, especially within architecture that is not newly built and where he is trying to sculpt something modern or timeless into it. He does this by framing and blocking these areas with materials used as a contrast or juxtaposition to the existing framework that he has to operate within.

> "It is a way for me to create a balance with something existing and outside my realm of control. I control it by having a 'box' or 'corner' put in, in another material. I call it a box or a corner because it's not just a decorative surface treatment but also about creating a volume and turning it into an architectural gesture within an environment."

He could create a similar effect by painting the space white – a "white cube" on which to project the new but prefers the atmospheric warmth of this form of material intervention.

The simplicity that Thulstrup generates in his spaces is not spare or empty. His simplicity is created through a tension of textures and the introduction of strong monolithic forms or planes. In order to achieve these tensions, he takes advantage of the conscious juxtaposition of material surfaces: compressed eelgrass panels and plate glass, for example, bird's eye birch veneer and white wool bouclé or natural pebble-dashed aggregate panels with sandblasted aluminium.

Interestingly, Thulstrup treats colour as a material mass in a similar manner. For example, he might add a monochrome custom-built chair lacquered in baby blue to one interior as a sculptural element, while incorporating planes of mint green wall panelling in another. But these are never mixed or jumbled around. They are never decorative and always "massive".

> "I am obsessed with material contrast. It is so important to have the right balance of raw and sleek; old and new. I think it's the way I highlight things. Because I work so much with my intuition, I have no recipe that I follow. I just strive to create a balance through contrast."

Sometimes he will use the materiality of a found or historical in-situ element, such as an ornate plaster ceiling or irregular exposed beams, to serve as hubs or axles to which he then fixes his environments. In the case of Peter's House (see page 29), this hub is the fragile primal materiality of the soil in the central atrium of the single-family home, planted as though it's a natural woodland. The powerful steel, glass, concrete, brick and solid wood materials of the house – and light, which is a massive material here too – are held in tension around the soil as if by some kind of centrifugal force, almost like a very tidy and heavy Cornelia Parker explosion.

Then there is the aspect of "honesty" that Thulstrup embraces in his use of materials. This ties back to the strength of Danish craft tradition and perhaps culture as well.

> "We are brought up with the idea that things have to be functional, and honesty is such an important part of that. For me, it starts with the material, with having a material to work with that is honest and true. It can sometimes be raw, sometimes it is a veneer, but it is what it is, and it is not trying to be something else. Honesty feeds through to the shape as well. A chair is a chair. It does not need anything more added to be that chair."

Honesty in design for Thulstrup goes hand in hand with utility and durability, as well as a rejection of materialism in terms of acquiring things without specific reason or necessity.

> "Utility is so important. We need to declutter our lives in so many ways. Things must have a purpose; they have to have a meaning and they have to be used. We must take away decorativeness for its own sake. Of course, an object can be both utilitarian and aesthetically pleasing but, I believe, it must have a purpose first."

Thulstrup's belief in sustainability also comes through his belief in quality and durability, two terms that belong together in his mind. He is very much aware of the responsibility inherent in creating and putting new objects into the world: "I would rather put products out there with a little more thought about how they are designed, and what materials are used to produce them so that they can live longer."

This way of working comes with a price tag in the first instance. Thus far, Thulstrup's projects tend to be very much at the luxury end of the market – not least because of the cost of the "honest" materials he tries to use when possible. There is nothing directly ostentatious or flashy about his work – his creations represent the luxury of quality and durability. "We can do prestigious things, but it is in a completely different way, using honesty and rawness," he says. By that, he means using certain materials in a massive way so that they are long-lasting.

But what is luxury in this context? Luxury is a strange word because it means so many things. It can represent wastefulness, exclusivity, and unfairness. For Thulstrup it has more positive connotations to do with feeling good, being generous, having space or the time and means to select things that resonate.

> "Luxury is not a bad word in itself, but it can very quickly become one, especially because it has a history of being misused. Well-made things are a luxury because it takes time to create them. Therefore, they become expensive, and as a result, they become precious and then only a few people can have them."

Luxury is also about reaching for things that people tend to not appreciate until they are gone: the luxury of time when your life is almost done; the luxury of untouched nature when we have destroyed so much of it; the luxury of delayed entropy in a 1,000-year-old tree or building. As illustrated by the popularity and success of the exclusive yet Walden-like, Noma restaurant (see page 77), people have an urge to experience an idea of enduring nature that is more than we are. We want to return to something natural and something that lasts, something that is built to be extraordinary for centuries. "Because of how we built it, I think Noma could very well be there for the next hundred years – as a building at least, probably not as a restaurant," says Noma co-owner René Redzepi. "Building things to last, having things that last a lifetime to pass on, is very luxurious."

Thulstrup also subscribes to this interpretation of luxury, it is an attitude that grows out of his belief in quality and durability.

> "I create environments that are luxurious, but they are not luxurious in a traditional way. Take a leather chair, for example. If the animal that the hide came from had a good life, and we use its skin to make a good chair, then that chair can last one hundred years. For me, that is luxury."

Thulstrup's respect for principles of form following function, honest materials, craftsmanship, simplicity and effectiveness, or even "less but better," does not run counter to many of the Bauhaus Modernist principles from a century ago, except perhaps the latter's prevailing preoccupation with novelty and technical innovation. Yet he leans even closer towards a connection with the functional traditionalism that is the essence of early to mid-twentieth century Danish design, which placed even more emphasis upon fine handcraft and high-quality materials. "Danish design is more luxurious than that of the Bauhaus," says Anne-Louise Sommer, Director of the Designmuseum Denmark.

> "It is more expensive to produce, because of the production process (craft) and more expensive natural materials. So, in that sense, you could say it is less radically functional. But maybe it is more radically functional when you look at it in terms of sustainability because it lasts for generations. It could also even be regarded as more radically functional because many people simply feel more comfortable being surrounded by natural materials."

Yet for all his love of massive materiality, one of the biggest juxtapositions Thulstrup likes to make is with the immaterial. His favourite intangible tangibles, light and time, have as much weight and texture in his work as the heaviest of stones.

> "I feel that a lot of people want to have tangible luxuries, but they don't need to be material in that way. Time is our most luxurious commodity today. It's about having that moment and being able to afford to take that moment, and it is also about being able to make the right choices."

J. Lindeberg
Stockholm, Sweden

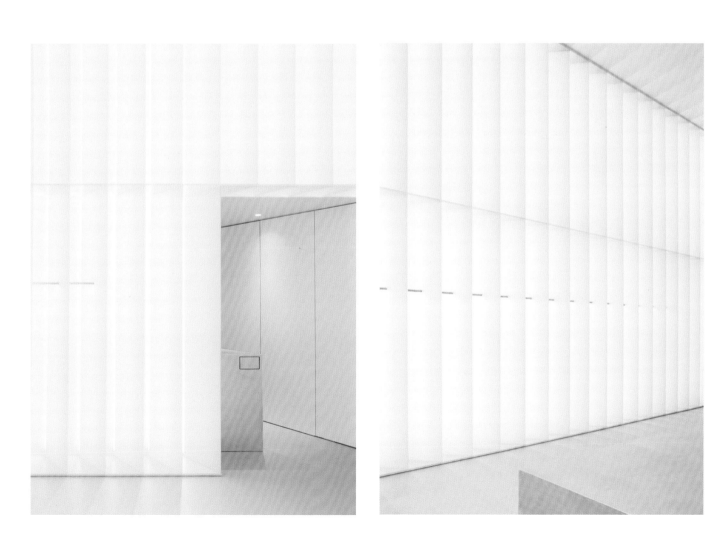

J. Lindeberg

Mark Kenly Domino Tan
Copenhagen, Denmark

Vipp Chimney House
Copenhagen, Denmark

Collage

Collage

Project: Retail
Dimensions: 175 square metres (1,883 sq ft)
Location: Aarhus, Denmark
Client: Group 88
Completed: November 2018

Collage is a multi-brand Danish fashion and accessories store that brings luxury brands such as Alexander McQueen, Balenciaga, Gucci, Loewe, Saint Laurent, and Valentino to the Scandinavian market. It belongs to Group 88, a family-owned luxury retailer founded in the 1980s and based in Copenhagen, which is now run by the third generation of owners, the brothers Thomas and Marius Møller. They approached David Thulstrup to create a distinctive backdrop of simplicity and style for their high-end products.

This outlet for women's accessories and clothing, located in Aarhus, is the second store designed by Thulstrup for Group 88. Like the previous men's store he designed for them in Illum, Copenhagen, this street-facing retail space contains original historic features that Thulstrup chose to highlight and balance by using his own strong, geometric volume designs, a palette of contemporary textures and a minimalist aesthetic.

The Collage women's store is housed in a former pharmacy and features large windows that look out onto one of the main streets in the old city centre. The space includes an original decoratively painted stucco ceiling, which has a colour palette of browns from rust to beige, gilded in places, and hand-painted panels with stylised floral motifs in pale blue. Thulstrup left this ceiling visible and created a dialogue with it using lighting and furniture volumes so that it complemented rather than competed with the merchandise.

Because the shop primarily sells shoes, handbags and smaller accessories from a range of designers – each with their own distinct visual identities – Thulstrup focused on creating a custom-made environment where the products could sit alongside each other. Ultimately the interior would be a neutral yet equal backdrop to these products that "played off their differences" in another level of dialogue. He achieved this in two ways: firstly, with a highly contemporary colour scheme that picks up on lighter elements of the historical ceiling and pulls them into the contemporary retail space. Secondly, by using broad, deceptively simple sculptural display elements in a statement colour, such as baby blue, high-gloss powder-coated steel, and contrasting them with matte chromatic grey shelving, counter and seating elements. Textured Steni wall panels with a grainy pebble aggregate surface add to the strong haptic sense, along with the large mirrors that are propped, seemingly carelessly, against the walls. The customer is instinctively pulled towards and into these surfaces – to touch them and experience them. A curved wall at the rear of the shop with a soft, pale grey matte render softens the powerful geometric forms, further guiding the customer through the shop towards the rear of the space, beyond the decorative ceiling. The strikingly long, straight tracks of parallel LED lighting serve a similar purpose.

Clever use of strong shadow gaps at the top and bottom of the massive baby-blue shelving units as well as at the bottoms of the beige pebble-dashed wall panels, makes them appear to float and brings a surprising lightness to the interior. Custom-built sofa elements with seats covered in a pastel pink bouclé fabric, along with a pale earth-toned fine wool rug, encourage customers to sit down, relax and spend time in the store.

Thulstrup designed two additional stores that year for Collage: both men's shops in Aarhus and Oslo. Together, all four outlets are fine examples of Thulstrup's skill at creating brand identity through deceptively simple mono-materiality and dialogue. It is the proportions of the custom furnishing elements and the textures of their surfaces that give an immediate sense of both the brand and quality without being overpowering or dominating. The interiors clearly belong together, and yet each one is individual and immediately identifiable thanks to the simple device of using a different signature highlight colour on the glossy shelf elements, whether it be baby blue, rich mustard yellow, powdery sage green or chromatic white.

Collage

←←
The material mood board for Collage combines textured pebble aggregate stone panels, pale grey matte clay render, wool bouclé rugs, matte grey steel and baby blue high-gloss powder-coated steel.

→
Simple and sculptural display elements, made from steel finished in a blue, high-gloss powder coating, are designed for the display of high-end products, as well as making a visual and spatial connection between the blue of the historic, richly detailed original ceiling, and the contemporary retail space.

↓
Throughout the store pale, textured, aggregate stone panel walls stand in contrast to the high-gloss geometric volumes of the display units. Floating below the historic ceiling, straight lines of light draw customers into the space.

→→
The textured matte finish of pebble aggregate wall panels absorbs light, whereas the high-gloss finish to the blue display elements reflects light throughout the space.

Site plan

Floor plan

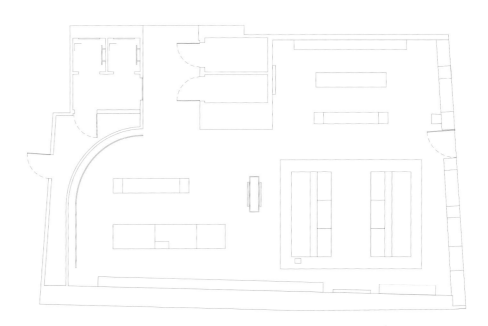

Collage

 ←↓
The colour palette was inspired by the original decorative ceiling. The high gloss pale blue which is used throughout for the display elements relates to the lightest part of the historic ceiling.

→
Simple and minimal light fittings are arranged in one direction throughout the shop and reinforce the linearity of the ultra-slim profiled wall shelves, as well as acting as a pathway pulling customers deep into the interior.

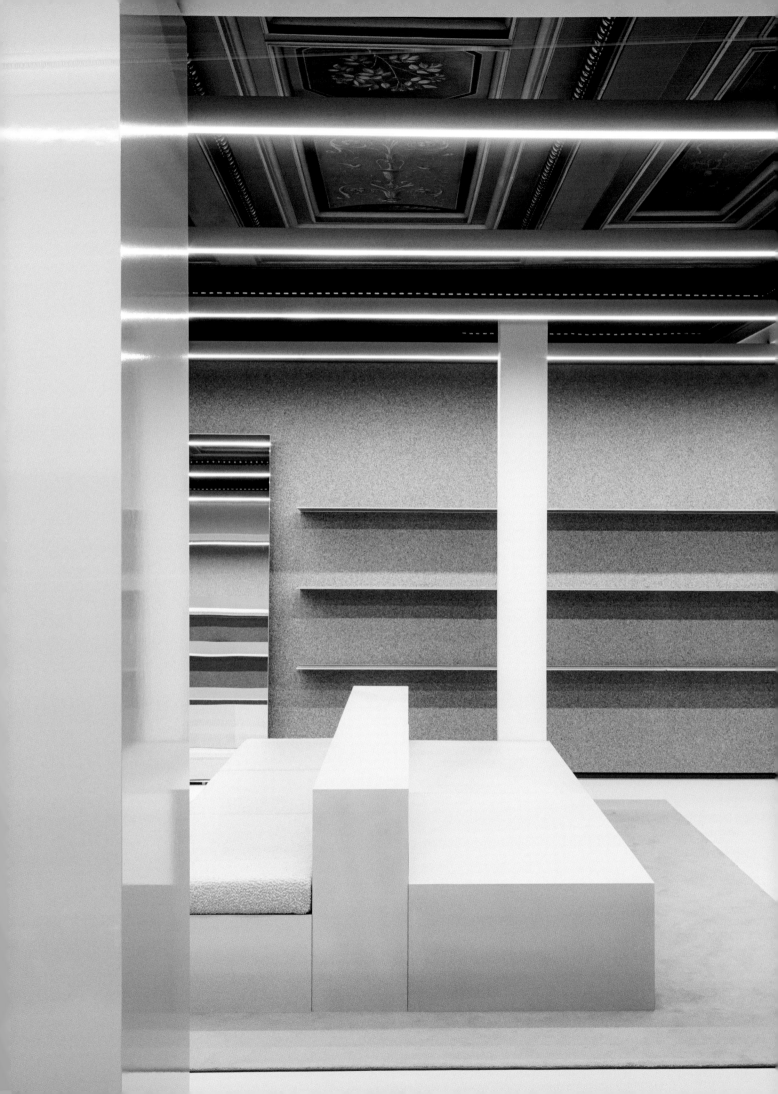

←
The earth-toned fine wool rugs, matte chromatic steel shelves and custom-built sofa elements in pale pink all reference the original historic ceiling.

↑
A detail view of the custom-built sofa elements which are upholstered in bouclé wool fabric.

→
Both the matte chromatic grey steel shelves and the stone aggregate wall panels absorb light, which serves to highlight products on display.

→→
The colours and classical detailing of the original panelled and painted ceiling are in dialogue with the sophisticated and minimalist aesthetic of the new store.

Collage

Collage Process

"This was my second Collage store – I had designed one previously in Copenhagen. The site was originally a pharmacy, and subsequently, a store for another clothing brand. There was nothing left that I could reuse, except – notably, as it became a central point of reference for the entire design – the painted ceiling that dated from the 1920s. Everything else was ripped out, with special measures taken to protect the ceiling before the construction got underway.

The first stage of the fit-out was installing the poured epoxy floor, which was critical to set the stage for all the other elements. Then the pebble-textured walls were installed, as well as furniture and shelving elements. I used bars of light hung below the historic ceiling to pull the old and new together, creating a holistic environment that is both timeless and contemporary.

I learned a lot developing the Collage retail programme, which involved working on three stores at the same time. Even though each store was different, I had to have a safe roll-out strategy that featured consistent shelving systems, millwork, joinery, and so on. So while I had the same underlying design identity throughout, each site brought its own challenges, so I had to react, create, learn and evolve all at the same time."

142

Over Time
Tiden Går

"We chase the sun here in Denmark. We chase the light because it is so precious."

The awareness and incorporation of the workings of time into David Thulstrup's oeuvre are a fascinating aspect of this still young designer's sensibility. His is an intuitive and fluid sense of time. There is a sensuality in the way he works with daylight as a temporal ingredient in terms of diurnal rhythms, how it moves through a space, or changes with the seasons. His love of hard-wearing materials means his work is nearly always built to endure over time as well. And his tendency to anchor a particular space as a meeting point of past, present and future through an existing historical detail or a local material – both from and of the earth – means he gives it a place in time and in the story of the world. "I think time is extremely beautiful," says Thulstrup:

> "Time is about understanding the correlation between the past, present and future. I always love to have these dashes of the past coming into where we are now. When I do interiors, it is very much about melting time in that place – different time zones that exist together. We have so much behind us, and so much in front of us and we are just here in this tiny bit of the present. What we surround ourselves with and what we do should in some ways entail all of it."

This view of a space, or place, as a nexus of time, is perhaps *the* pivotal element of Thulstrup's architectural work. He speaks more often about materiality, but when he does, it is almost always as a means to express the passing of time. "I don't want to be trendy; I want to create things that endure," he says. This is important to Thulstrup in both his design language and the choices he makes in precious and robust materials. He also consciously chooses materials for how they bear witness to the passing of time – changing and becoming more beautiful as they get older.

In the reception lounge of the Noma restaurant (see page 82), for example, Thulstrup used natural or vegetable-tanned leather for the bench sofas despite, or rather because of, the heavy use a restaurant interior is subjected to. With pale, natural leather

upholstery, "the first spill is a disaster, but after five hundred spills, it is beautiful", he says. What Thulstrup is interested in is the patina that will develop on the material through use. It was a decision with which Noma chef René Redzepi was initially unconvinced as he worried, understandably, about the stretch of time between that first spill and the five hundredth.

> "There is always a little bit of a battle between the vision and the reality. As a person that is going to be there every day, you also need to think practically as well. Will it actually work? Will this material last? That is always the most annoying bit for many architects and designers. It's so beautiful but will this door last being shut one hundred times a day, or will we have to redo it every six months?"

Thulstrup's use of hard-wearing, hard-working materials has stood the test of time thus far. "I think it's working well," says Redzepi. "I can't say there are any parts of our restaurant that are not 110 per cent." Natural leather that patinates with age is a material element that Thulstrup also used for the Font chairs he designed in 2018 for the Danish furniture company Møbel (see page 227). He was already planning ahead for the lounge chairs' future lives as antiques when he specified Dunes leather upholstery to go with the polished steel frames. "I can't wait to see these chairs in fifteen years' time," he says, "because they will have completely changed and acquired their own unique patinas from fingerprints, drops of whisky or splashes of coffee – they will only become more beautiful with time."

Working with time past and future histories in this way goes hand in hand with Thulstrup's use of "honest" materials. "This sense of time through a patina making something more beautiful with age only really works with natural materials," he says.

"Cheap white laminate furniture, such as shelves or tables, are the most lifeless objects that you can look at. They are just dead, white, non-interchangeable things. When they get older, you just see damage and dirt, and it's not pretty!" At the time of writing, Thulstrup was in the process of having a desk made from solid Swedish granite for his own apartment. It is not yet completed and he is already thinking about how it will look when he is an old man. "It's going to show the marks of where I have rested my forearms on it over the years. I love that", he says.

Thulstrup would never introduce a historical decorative object or material for theatrical effect, or as a superficial expression of connection to place or time, like a souvenir or memento. Rather, he embeds that connection through the materials he uses. Looking ahead to the future as his commissions shift to entire architectural projects – outsides as well as insides – he is drawn increasingly towards working with salvaged materials. "I would happily use bricks salvaged from an old house to build a new house, or salvaged wood for a floor if appropriate." Unfortunately the supply of recycled building materials is still limited, but the demand for these materials is expanding rapidly, especially with the global materials shortages that are causing problems worldwide in terms of both cost and availability, thus the market will follow, believes Thulstrup. He sees the use of recycled materials not just as a more environmentally-friendly way of building, but as an integration of time in another form – as something precious.

Thulstrup believes the introduction of historical – or new – decorative objects is an imposed form of storytelling that he is averse to since it contradicts the honesty or the "truth" of a location.

> "I don't try to create customer journeys to specific destinations. I try to take what is already there and add my vision to it. I tell the story of the place – or rather, I design from that knowledge. When I start a project, I always try to dive into its history and then make sure it is present in some form. Not in an exaggerated, comical fashion but in a small or understated way. I always want to find the narrative that gives things a meaning or purpose."

It is the story of a place that interests Thulstrup, in the service of his quest to bring balance through that time nexus. It is also a very holistic and rational approach. He is currently working on the design of a summer house in the north of Denmark, for example, and the narrative he is following for that is about how to work with the nearby pine forest, the stones and pebbles that are on the plot, the driftwood that gets washed up on the beach, or the slope of the hill or the view. "With my design", he says, "I am trying to create a narrative based on all those elements alongside the wishes of the client." This means that when he chooses materials, it is for a reason, not just because he thought they were nice.

Another large project he and his team are currently working on is five, very different, very old buildings in Copenhagen that need to be merged together for a retail project. "I want the customer to still understand the original individual rooms. I want people entering the space to understand that it is not a typical retail experience but something that has been here for three hundred years. I'm just there to add on the next level of time – I'm not there to cover it all up for the sake of brand positioning", he explains.

There is one more timeline of storytelling that goes hand-in-hand with that of local materials and historical features, and it is the one of craftsmanship – the design, quality and precision of joints in a dining chair, for example. The Arv chair (see page 218), designed by Thulstrup and made by Brd Krüger, literally carries the history of the joiner's art in its arms. "Danish design is long-lasting, or timeless, for two reasons," says Anne-Louise Sommer of the Designmuseum Denmark. "It is built on tradition and the redesign of old typologies and because of good craftsmanship and materials." It is a form of storytelling that comes with a hefty price tag but stretched across a lifetime, or even two or three, of use, like patina, it begins to take on a different value.

After World War II, Denmark was one of the few countries in the world actively preserving its fine craft tradition, especially with respect to furniture. Parallel to international modernism, a new functionalist furniture school, led by the architect Kaare Klint, was emerging in Denmark. But instead of breaking with history, this movement embraced it, rejecting industrialisation in favour of handcraft in a manner not dissimilar to the Arts and Crafts movement almost a century earlier in Britain. Klint actively sent his pupils to the design museum to study older furniture and apply what they learned to their new designs. These new designs should build on historical typologies, improving them for contemporary life. "Klint had a famous saying: 'A chair should be of a good old family'", says Sommer, "and with it he advocated for a continuous craft tradition. Danish design is about refining existing ideas from other ages and cultures. It's not about innovation or revolution – it's more about an evolutionary approach." Even when Danish design did become more industrialised, with technological improvements after 1950 these craft qualities continued to be incorporated into the industrially-aided designs.

The natural passage of time as our planet completes its wobbly elliptical revolutions around the sun is marked in the changing seasons. Located 56 degrees north, Denmark is in the higher latitudes of the temperate zone. This means that there are big seasonal fluctuations in the amount of sunlight it gets. In winter, the days are very short, around seven hours, and the sun is weak. In summer, the days are very long, around seventeen hours, and at the time of the summer solstice, it never really gets properly dark. Add to this the country's maritime climate, and you get cold and dark winters and light summers with unpredictable weather. The country's climate and seasons define the form of Danish domestic architecture. "Up here in the north, there is a real difference between inside and out," says Thulstrup. "We don't live in a climate where we can have open boundaries between indoor and outdoor spaces. Our windows have to be really well insulated!"

When he is designing in Denmark, Thulstrup always has the path of the sun in mind and is always trying to optimise access to sunlight. His team do light studies for different times of year for every project – a task made far easier these days thanks to new technologies – there are even phone apps to track daylight at any given time of year. In Danish Modernist and contemporary residential architecture, the buildings are often low-slung, like the landscape, and tend to have large windows to pull in as much daylight as possible, as well as to provide a feeling of porosity between outside and inside, and between home, nature and that beloved but infrequent guest – the sun. "We chase the sun here in Denmark because it is so precious. There is a necessity to cater for moments when you can't be outside. So how do we cater for it? How do we find that gesture?" asks Thulstrup. He does this by finding ways to bring the outside in, and vice versa, through sight axes and openings. He also considers vistas in his designs by creating dialogues and context. In this way, for example, a wall in a garden, standing away from a house, can still be part of the interior architectural experience when viewed through the window. The levels of engagement between what it is that you look at from the inside out and how you resonate with bringing the outside in is something that Thulstrup tries hard to work with and balance in his architecture, so that the living experience is not just perceived as an interior one.

This consideration for connections with nature and seasonality through design was also of high importance in the design of the Noma interior (see pages 77–107). The very essence of the restaurant's cuisine is seasonal. In the winter months, the menu is more reliant on the bounty of the sea, and in the summer, the bounty of the land. Allowing seasonal ingredients to lead the menu is reflected in the styling of the decor and tableware by Noma's own stylist, Christine Rudolph, who changes the decor, mostly with natural found and foraged materials, in harmony with each season. Thulstrup specifically designed the solid material baseline to accommodate seasonal change within the restaurant. Right outside Noma's doors are both sea and land: Piet Oudolf's romantic, yet also functional kitchen garden provides ingredients for the table as well as magnificent seasonal displays of subtle colour variations that connect the restaurant's buildings to the water's edge and the sky above.

This harmony of inside and outside, seasonally driven cuisine, landscaping, architecture and styling, natural and artificial light, cooking, working, eating and enjoying is all held together by the forms and materials of Thulstrup's interior, but also by his sensibility for the passage of time as part of the storytelling. As Redzepi notes:

> "One of the most important things that David contributed is that he drew in this giant window at the one end of the restaurant space. That was actually a huge structural change to the whole building. It was a controversial thing back then with the architects, but Noma without that huge window would not have been Noma."

One of Denmark's most famous painters is Vilhelm Hammershøi (1864–1916). He is particularly known for his paintings of domestic interiors that are nearly empty. Despite occasional guest appearances in these interiors by his wife Ida, the main character in his work is daylight. Hammershøi was an absolute master of the soft, cool greyscale palette of a low, northern sun filtering through mist or clouds and windows into a room. His portrayal of light is so physical it is almost material. In the context of the equally cool, understated palette of blues, greys and chromatic whites of his Copenhagen home, where he tended to paint, it is also considered to be quintessentially Danish.

There is another kind of light, artificial light, that is also considered so Danish that it has helped give the world its favourite, and rather overused, Danish word: *hygge*. *Hygge* means a feeling of cosy and contented conviviality, and it applies specifically to interior environments engineered to elicit that feeling with the use of candles, lamps and furnishings. "In many ways you can see Hammershøi as the antithesis to *hygge*", says Anne-Louise Sommer. "His interiors are beautiful and sublimely aesthetical, but at the same time, they are austere, even slightly alienated, with almost no traces of human life. *Hygge*, on the other hand, is a rather chaotic, very personal take on the human-made environment we call a home."

In Denmark, sunlight is a soft and gentle friend, a physical presence to be welcomed and treasured when it deigns to turn up, but artificial light, supplied by candles and electric lights, is equally treasured in combination with the right furnishings where it elicits feelings of cosiness. The creation of *hygge* is an artform absolutely essential to human wellbeing during long, dark Nordic winters. It is also an indispensable juxtaposition to the long daylight months of summer. Thus, this seasonal dialogue between natural and artificial light is a defining force in Danish architecture as well as interiors.

"I am so happy to have been born up here in a place where we have seasons", says Thulstrup. "We grow up with massive contrasts in terms of light, and learning how to navigate the big changes that result from that has a big impact on who we are." Despite having a strong dislike of filling interiors with objects and "things" generally associated with the feeling of *hygge*, Thulstrup is completely at home with the dichotomy of natural and artificial light as a shaper of architecture and interiors from season to season, as well as from night to day. He has also had a great deal of experience with manipulating light in order to create specific atmospheres. He works a lot with artificial and natural light in his projects to induce a sense of seasons or time of day and other atmospheres indoors, using spots as wayfinders, for example, to navigate the space, or hiding light sources in a surface. "It's a real science", he says, "and over the years, I have worked with some great specialists and lighting companies that I have learned a great deal from along the way."

Working with natural light and shadows as if they were materials that tie together inside and outside and make the passing of time a tangible experience is clearly one of Thulstrup's favourite preoccupations. He always tends to choose the natural over the object-bound artificial when he can. "When I work archi-tecturally, I try to work with views through interiors because there is nothing more beautiful than what happens when daylight comes through a window and hits something," he says. Deciding what he wants that natural light to hit is important: should it hit the floor or a wall, or should it continue, cleaving a slow-moving path through the space? Then, of course, there are the shadows to consider too. Thulstrup is not a strong believer in installing massive windows, preferring to use smaller windows to filter the light into a space. "Because light is also about shadows; the differentiation between shadows and light in a space is vital", he adds. A good example of this is Vester Voldgade (see page 167), Thulstup's 2020 renovation of a loft apartment in an 1890s building in Copenhagen. The original space had limited natural light, so he opened it up and added strategically located window openings that allowed daylight to become part of the definition of the volumes without flooding the space.

Thulstrup's own personal *hygge* moments of well-being also tend to come from creating natural and temporary moments for himself. That's not to say that he does not love candles as much as the next Dane, just that he appreciates working and moving with – not against – the daylight to create junctures where he gives himself the luxury of moments in time to bask in that light or simply appreciate its presence. It is an appre-ciation Thulstrup has much in common with his ancestral countryman Hammershøi.

"During the winter, when the sun is shining, the sunlight bounces off a building across the road into a corner of our apartment for about thirty minutes right at the end of the day," says Thulstrup. "So, of course, I keep a chair in that spot because at the end of a dark winter work day it is the most lovely place to sit and catch a moment of sun on your skin."

Collage
Aarhus, Denmark

Vipp Loft
Copenhagen, Denmark

Vipp Loft

&Tradition
Aarhus, Denmark

162 &Tradition

Collage
Oslo, Norway

Vester Voldgade

Vester Voldgade

Project:	Residential
Dimensions:	125 square metres (1,345 sq ft)
Location:	Copenhagen, Denmark
Client:	Private
Completed:	January 2020

In 2019, a couple acquired the roof space above their cramped top-floor apartment in the heart of Copenhagen and asked David Thulstrup to transform it architecturally. An abundance of natural light and space is one of the greatest luxuries in central Copenhagen, so the primary goal in Thulstrup's architectural conversion of this private apartment in an 1890s building was to let the light in and create a greater sense of volume. Thanks to the additional attic space, through a series of radical interventions, he was able to remove the ceiling and open the rooms up to, and through, the roof.

At the core of the new apartment volume is a bright, double-height living area with exposed rafters. To enhance the new sense of light and openness, the original arched windows in the living area were elongated, and new windows were installed into the roofline on the street side. The only dividing walls in the apartment enclose the two bedrooms and two bathrooms.

The airy living space, with its exposed beams, cedes directly into the open-plan, single-height kitchen and dining area towards the rear of the building. This area then ends with a set of large bi-folding glass doors that lead to a terrace – a further extension of the room – allowing daylight to flood in. Another key intervention was to create the roof structure for a second upstairs terrace over the ceiling of the open kitchen below.

Typical of Thulstrup, the sense of space in the apartment was underscored and increased as much by the materials as the volumes. Wood, stone and metal were used with extraordinary consideration and maximum simplicity. Although Thulstrup is not always a fan of plain white walls, the colour was an essential unifier to both accentuate the angles created by the roofline and offset features such as the exposed timber rafters of the lofty space. Double-width heart oak Dinesen floorboards run throughout the main living area, boosting both scale and lightness and bringing a very subtle luxury to match the light pouring in through the windows.

In keeping with the restrained use of materials, Thulstrup used his brushed aluminium Plate cabinets, designed for Reform, for the kitchen cupboards, island bench and wardrobes. The primary bathroom and a guest bathroom are lined in speckled pinkish-brown Bornholm granite.

The only extrovert material and formal detail in the apartment is the statement-making spiral staircase leading from the main living area up to a mezzanine above the kitchen. It was custom-made from glass-blasted steel with a yellow-electroplated zinc finish that has iridescent dashes of green, pink and blue. This surface comes alive when the sun shines, reflecting and creating shadow plays within the living area

To keep the clutter of furniture to a minimum, Thulstrup designed a built-in bench sofa in the living space that runs the length of one wall, another custom-built sofa in a TV nook, a desk, and a platform bed and bedhead, all from the same oak as the flooring. A dining nook opposite the kitchen is also fitted out with a customised banquette seat covered in vegetable leather that will develop a patina with age.

←←
The material mood board for Vester Voldgade combines brushed aluminium, massive heart oak planks, Danish granite from the island of Bornholm, natural leather and glass-blasted steel with a yellow-electroplated zinc finish.

→
In the entrance space, white walls unify the space and make connections to the other key surface treatments used throughout the interior – oak and brushed aluminium.

↓
The living area sits in a double height volume with exposed structural timber elements. Natural light is introduced through elongated arched windows, and a bespoke built-in sofa occupies the length of one wall.

→→
In the living area, the key spatial and material characteristics are brought together to create an airy open floor plan in the double-height space under the steeply-angled roof. A spiral staircase connects the living space with a mezzanine guest room above.

Site plan

Section

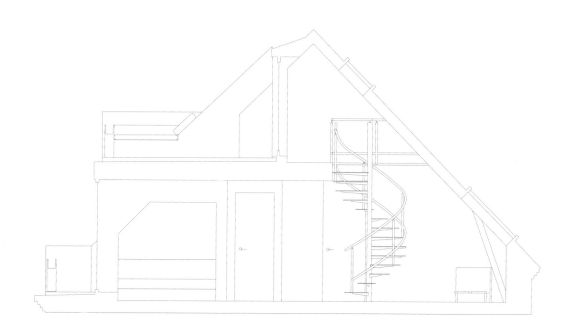

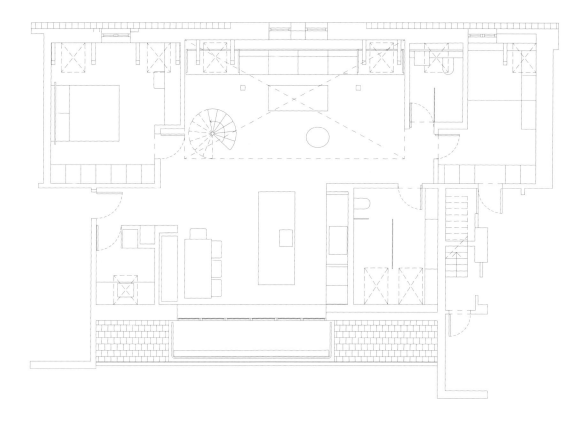

Lower level
plan

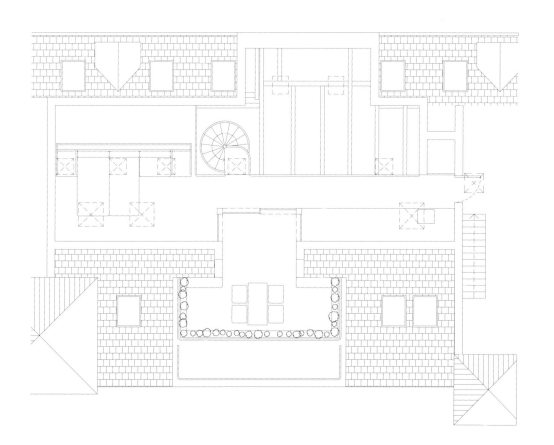

Upper level
plan

Vester Voldgade

↑
The open-plan kitchen features brushed aluminium
counters and cabinetry, as well as large bi-folding glass
doors that open onto the terrace.

→
A detail view of the dining area where a custom-designed
pendant lamp creates a point of focus, and the natural
leather upholstery will patinate over time.

→→
In the kitchen, David Thulstrup's Plate kitchen, designed
for Danish company Reform, a full height wall of brushed
aluminium doors opens to reveal the oven and hob.
The island counter, fitted with doors in the same finish,
is topped with sheet stainless steel, which presents an
uninterrupted surface aside from the integrated sink
and simple pillar tap.

Vester Voldgade

←
In the living room, the original wood structure stands in contrast to the smoothness of the heart oak floor-boards and brushed aluminium in the kitchen beyond.

↑→
The main bathroom features a bespoke handbasin in red speckled Bornholm granite combined with the same brushed aluminium used in the kitchen as well as for joinery throughout the apartment.

←↓
The spiral staircase, made from glass-blasted steel with a yellow plated zinc finish, leads from the living space to the mezzanine level.

→
The original arched windows were elongated to create appropriately proportioned windows for the double height living room which was created by removing the ceiling and incorporating the old loft space into the new apartment.

↑
A light-filled mezzanine accommodating a guestroom
and a terrace above the kitchen was created by convert-
ing a previously enclosed attic space.

←→
In the main bedroom on the lower floor, wide heart oak
planks are used both for the floors and a floating desk.
Brushed aluminium panels with push-catches open to
reveal floor-to-ceiling wardrobes.

Vester Voldgade
Process

"The site had incredible potential, but when I first saw it, it was dark and broken up into lots of very small rooms. The clients had purchased the attic space above their apartment with a plan to somehow connect the two. They had seen what I had achieved at Noma and entrusted me with the task of unravelling their rather warren-like home and giving it a new lease of life.

The three-dimensional spatial design was the biggest challenge. I had to open up the volume to bring in natural light, and introduce connections between the various parts of the accommodation programme. The whole roof was scaffolded to protect the site and the double height volume stripped out. It was at this stage that the old wooden beams revealed themselves. They held so much character and history, I knew they would make a unique contribution to the end result.

One of the most satisfying aspects of the construction was the level of detail I was able to achieve. I worked with very high-end finishes and detailing, as well as bespoke furniture. The kitchen seating, the kitchen itself, the built-in sofa, the workbench and the electroplated stair were all custom-designed and enabled me to work with, and learn from, some of the best craftspeople in Denmark."

Sensibility
Følsomhed

"I am an emotional person; I need that to create."

I first met David Thulstrup in January 2016 when I travelled to Copenhagen to do a story on his design for Peter's House (see page 29). I remember being struck by his kindness and gentle solicitude. He seemed to have thought about everything I might need for the story and had planned my stay meticulously. I was also struck, not by his ambition, but by the fact that he so clearly seemed to know where he wanted to go professionally. He appeared to have a plan, and my arrival in Copenhagen was part of it.

Thulstrup's first big interior architecture job was with Jean Nouvel, one of the world's most prominent architects. His second big job was with Peter Marino, one of, if not *the* most famous interior architect in the Western fashion and art worlds. Thulstrup's first major client was one of the biggest retailers in China. His first house got him a full feature in *Wallpaper* magazine, which was the article I had visited him to write, an achievement that many architects don't ever get to cross off their bucket lists – even Scandinavian ones. His first set of retail interiors was for Georg Jensen. His first restaurant design was for the world's best restaurant. His first bar stools broke completely with the classic typology (Tank, see page 214) and had their debut at an e15 reception in the Bar Basso in Milan during the annual Salone del Mobile season. The Tank stools won a 2021 Monocle Design award and are now a permanent feature at Bar Basso – a rare, if not unique, honour for a contemporary designer.

Such milestones in the first fourteen years of Thulstrup's career are consistent in terms of a driven trajectory. He sought and found the best teachers for what he wanted to do, developed his own design language, cut his professional teeth in the extremely tough world of fashion retail, and then sought and found the kind of clients that he wanted to work with. How did he manage that, and where does he intend to go next?

So far, we have looked at Thulstrup's sensibility towards place, time and materials, but perhaps his biggest superpower, if he

has one, comes from his sensibility towards people and his surroundings. He has the ability to listen very closely and empathise; by focusing fully on what people are saying and feeling he is very good at imagining himself in their shoes and understanding their needs. It may sound a little mundane, but this focused social ability generates very precise observations, which he then uses to translate into his designs – to which people react so warmly in return.

This final chapter is necessarily a more personal one because his sensitivity also applies to himself; for example, how he wants to work and what he hopes to achieve. It will explore how his work begins with people and within himself, and then sets it in the perspective of his career thus far. Tony Chambers, the former editor-in-chief of *Wallpaper* magazine observes:

> "When I first met David Thulstrup, it was at the beginning of his trajectory. I found him to be so quietly engaging and refreshingly modest. His architecture and design are outstanding, but there is a modesty about that too, which I guess is what all great design – all long-lasting design – has."

Farah Ebrahimi and her partner, Philipp Mainzer of e15, first met Thulstrup by chance at the Milan Furniture Fair in 2018. She says of Thulstrup:

> "It ended up being the beginning of an inspiring partnership between us. For Philipp and I, it is essential that we share a chemistry and that our conversations evolve. David has a sense of humour and openness that we very much appreciate. He is extremely calm, kind, open and sharing in his approach and his general character."

Following their first meeting, Ebrahimi and Mainzer visited Thulstrup to discuss the production of some bespoke barstools he had designed for Gasoline Grill in Copenhagen. They ended up making Thulstrup's Tank bar stools for the project and later added them to the e15 collection, which was by no means a given. "We don't just pick and choose or brief designers when we make a new product," says Ebrahimi. "We look for good conversations, similar values and understanding of what is essential. [...] We always take the long view and try to develop lasting relationships with designers and architects."

Thulstrup and e15's Tank barstool ended up being a lockdown creation. It was produced between 2019 and 2020 during the Covid-19 pandemic and did not get the standard launch on a trade fair stand but made its debut in 2021 in Milan's most famous bar instead. "Maurizio [Stocchetto], the owner of Bar Basso, is a long-time friend and supporter of design companies," says Ebrahimi. "When we asked him if we could launch the Tank barstool at his place, he said, 'yes, of course!'"

This collaboration with e15 may have been atypical for them, but it is typical for Thulstrup. He designed a set of barstools as part of an interior, and then chose the perfect furniture company to make them. They not only agreed but went on to put them into production and presented them at one of the world's most famous bars. As with his other successful projects, this happened not just because of what Thulstrup designs, but how he does it.

> "I have always been good at reading a room, at sensing people's moods. It means I have a kind of precognition when I am designing about what it will be like to come into a room, what the atmosphere will be like and then think about what I can do to change that – if it needs changing. I appreciate that it is a gift to be able to talk to everybody and to be able to tune myself into other people, be they clients or friends, artists or craftspeople, millionaires or not."

Thulstrup's design of the Noma interiors for René Redzepi happened in an exceptionally short time span and was a fine collaborative balancing act with the owners, architects, craftspeople and others all the way down the line. One part of the design brief was to select the right dining chairs. Thulstrup responded by designing the bespoke Arv dining chairs for the restaurant himself. Says Redzepi of the process:

> "That chair was, for me, a fantastic example of us working together on something. There were some clear things that we asked for: a handmade chair that was not to be found anywhere else; a chair that represented Scandinavian design vision, but that felt fresh."

Ask any architect, the task of getting the balancing act right between the client, contractors, craftspeople and the project itslef takes a great deal of skill, and it is one that Thulstrup is well equipped for.

> "I am extremely solution-oriented. I am good at explaining what I want, and I'm also very uncompromising when I need to be. I am also good at listening to the proposals of clients, craftspeople or builders so they feel engaged in being part of finding that solution. It is very much about the way in which you deliver a message to the client, so that they feel part of the decision rather than being imposed upon."

This is an approach Thulstrup tries hard to implement with his own team as well. He was an astute observer whilst working for Jean Nouvel's studio and then Peter Marino in the early days of his career. He noted that their studios worked best – and the staff produced their best work – when motivated by direct contact and feedback from Nouvel and Marino, respectively. "I always want my team to feel that they can come to me with ideas," says Thulstrup. "I know where I want to go, and within that process, it's my role to help them get to the same place." This does not mean to say that Thulstrup believes he is infallible.

> "Of course, I sometimes see something and think, 'oh shit, that was a bad idea, David.' Part of being creative is that you have to experiment, but as I get older, I have more experience in knowing what the right solution is. It's also about having the confidence to say, yes or no."

In autumn 2019 Thulstrup went out to California for a few days to meet with art collectors Mei and Allan Walburg and discuss the redesign of the interior of the winery on their Donum Estate in Sonoma County (see page 204). Danish-born Allan is one of the owners of the Bestseller Fashion Group China, which Thulstrup designed a number of retail interior concepts for earlier in his career, and is, therefore, a client he had worked with for some time. This project, however, was a far more personal one, as it was situated in the couple's biodynamic, organic vineyard that is also home to a large part of their significant art collection. (The Donum Sculpture Park contains artworks by Louise Bourgeois, Zhan Wang, Elmgreen & Dragset, Yue Minjun, Olafur Eliasson and Keith Haring, amongst others.)

"David is interested in understanding what it is that you actually want," says Allan, "and from that, he designs the functionality. This, I feel, is one of the differences between him and many other architects who tend to have a lot of ideas about everything. I think it is important for them to have their own ideas about creativity and style, because that's what they should have, but when it comes to functionality, they shouldn't be teaching us about what it is we need."

Throughout 2022, Thulstrup was also in the process of designing a private house for the Warburgs in San Francisco, so he and the couple have spent many hours discussing both their new residence and his designs for the Donum Estate wine tasting and reception rooms. Chinese-born Mei also says she appreciates the way that Thulstrup does not impose his ideas but listens first and asks a lot of questions. She says they have talked a lot about the philosophy of feng shui and her related aversion to cold materials and sharp corners, for example. "Unlike many others, who tend to keep a distance when they are not familiar with such things, I feel David is always keenly interested and really wants to know and understand."

For Thulstrup, the client relationship and the project always start with two very basic questions: "Who is the client?" and "What is the building?"

"There are so many homogenous designs out there that don't take into consideration *where* they are and *who* they are built for. I have my creative standpoint, and my role is always to try to diversify and create variations within it because I am working for different people."

In other words, architecture is as much about culture as it is about aesthetics and taste. It is all but impossible for an architect or designer to put themselves in somebody else's shoes culturally, but they can pay careful attention to the client's needs and preferences and then put them before their own. "It is vital for the designer to understand which colour schemes, which material palettes, and which types of stone and wood can work. Only after that can I start applying my aesthetic point of view", adds Thulstrup.

Being the committed designer that he is, Thulstrup uses all his senses to listen, feel, empathise and learn, and then he uses these inputs to generate creative output through layers of dialogues: with people, with spaces, with materials and with himself. The first and most important dialogue in this respect, Thulstrup believes, is the one that he has with himself:

"This is the internal dialogue about what it is I want to achieve or realise. The dialogues that you have with yourself in between, when you are not actively working on a project, are just as important as the work process because those are the moments of reflection when you can step back a little. I am getting better and better at understanding the function of this internal dialogue process and enjoying it more and more. Doubt is a really important part of it, of course, as is knowing when to let go of that doubt."

The second layer of dialogue is the one Thulstrup has with his team in terms of how he wants them to work with, and for him, what they should spend time on and how they can contribute as well as feel that they are contributing.

> "I am a very open person, but I can also be very clear about what not to waste time on. I think everybody can rise to the occasion; everybody has a talent. Sometimes the most interesting staff conversations happen across the lunch table, when someone shows me the work of an architect I haven't seen or talks about an exhibition they have seen. I think those kinds of dialogues are very important to have too."

Despite a growing number of projects coming in, Thulstrup has a deliberately small team these days of around fourteen staff members, and that team size dictates the number of projects he chooses to accept at any given time. The size of the team is in direct correlation with finding the correct balance between contemplation and dialogue. "I don't want to work on a lot of projects at the same time because I don't want to lose that connection," he says. "It's also why I know that I will never have a large office – because a lot of the things that I do are based on the understanding that comes through human interaction." His practice method is to keep the team tight and close so that he can completely entrust parts of the work to them, freeing him up more for his inner creative dialogues. It's an interesting conscious decision that is also quite contemporary in its attitude to growth where the importance of finding the right balance between quality of life (your life, your client's life, your team's lives) and the quality of work you produce takes precedence. Bigger is not necessarily better.

The third important layer of dialogue for Thulstrup is the dialogue he has with his clients. He has now reached a level of experience and standing that means clients listen to what he has to say and respect his opinion. When he discusses projects with them he listens closely and carefully to what they are telling him they are looking for and then explains his thoughts and ideas in a clear and considered manner. Communication is key:

> "I am not accustomed to using words that can feel alienating to people who are not necessarily part of that language. Therefore, I can make my vision understandable to people who don't necessarily have an architectural language that they can relate to."

Apart from the more abstract dialogues Thulstrup also conducts with materials, landscapes, places and time, there is one other very vital interlocutor in his life, and that is his partner of nine years, the artist Martin Jacob Nielsen:

> "I think David is wiser than he maybe makes himself out to be. It takes many years of experience and an open heart to be able to put yourself in other people's shoes and truthfully say, 'Yes, I get you; I see what you mean; I understand.' He relates to the physical world in this way too. This, I believe, is David's great strength."

Thulstrup and Nielsen are a partnership and team and their dialogues with one another are another significant point of influence on Thulstrup's creative process. "I respect his creative opinion so much", says Thulstrup of Nielsen:

> "We are two creatives together, but as an artist, his creative work is boundary-less, whereas my world is filled with boundaries that I must navigate within. So, in some ways, we have different viewpoints on what creativity is, but the dialogue that comes out of it is absolutely beautiful."

This questing sensibility of Thulstrup's to both people and his surroundings that Nielsen talks about is a powerful tool, but it can also be highly draining on the psyche. One of the biggest learning curves for someone whose creative force is driven in that way can be how to use it without using up your own internal reserves. "I think I am a very intuitive creator. Even when I don't exactly know where I am going, I always have an intuition that pulls me in a particular direction," says Thulstrup. He treasures his sensitivity and intuition but has also learned over time that they come from a more fragile part of his psyche that needs to be protected. So he has learned to narrow his internal aperture to the world and filter out the input when necessary. It is also perhaps part of the reason why he has found that he works best with a small team and focuses on projects where he feels his talents can best be applied. He explains:

> "If you are very open, you also take so much in that you then end up having to navigate through it all to find the right things. So sometimes it pays to be the opposite. Being sensitive is also about being in the right environment. You need the right environment in order for sensitivity to come out as creativity."

Thulstrup has now reached a point in his career where he no longer needs to prove anything. His body of work to date, not to mention the numerous awards he has received, do that for him, and he is justifiably proud of the spaces and buildings he has created. He has also "arrived" within himself – he knows who he is, and what he likes and does not like. He is the first to admit that each of the people and projects he has encountered on his career journey thus far have contributed to who he is, to how he wants to create and what is important to him. Now, he feels, is the time to look to where he wants to go next on this journey he has navigated with such focus and determination thus far.

> "These are beautiful projects, and I am really proud of them. They are examples of, and part of, my own storytelling. Everything I have collected here from the last fourteen years is what I am building the future on. With this book, I want to show where I am heading and what it is that I stand for. This is where I am now: sharpening my senses."

Garde Hvalsøe
Copenhagen, Denmark

David's Apartment
Copenhagen, Denmark

David's Apartment

The Donum Estate
Sonoma, California, USA

The Donum Estate

Furniture

Designed: 2018
Producer. Møbel Copenhagen
Materials: Ceramic, steel

The Pair Side Tables are, as their name suggests, a pairing of handcrafted ceramic tables in clay and a high-gloss glaze finish, with a contrasting taller steel table. The tables can stand alone or in groups, with a variety of combinatory possibilities.

Pair Side Table

Designed: 2021
Producer: Søuld
Materials: Tinted glass, polished steel, eelgrass

The Momentum Low Table belongs to a collection of four limited-edition designs that explore the tactility, warmth and acoustic properties of eelgrass mats. The table juxtaposes the coarse grain of the eelgrass used for the legs, with two smooth surfaces: one a hand-polished steel plate that reflects light onto a layer of tinted glass above.

Momentum Low Table

Designed: 2021
Producer: e15
Materials: European oak, steel

Crafted in European oak, the Tank Bar Stool was originally designed for the Gasoline Grill restaurant in Copenhagen and later put into production by German furniture producer e15. The sculptural piece is a simple silhouette combining mono-materiality with a timeless design.

Tank Bar Stool

Designed: 2020
Producer: Sørensen Leather
Materials: Leather, polished steel

The Landscape collection consists of three limited-edition designs. The table is characterised by its hand-polished steel legs with simple L-profiles. The table surface is made from a natural pale leather that is soft to the touch. A concealed drawer, located within the thickness of the tabletop, is lined in light blue leather that contrasts with the pink of the outer surface.

Landscape Table

Designed: 2018
Producer: Brdr. Krüger
Materials: European oak, Danish paper cord

The Arv Chair was designed especially for Noma restaurant. The chair rearticulates the history of classic Danish dining chairs and is handcrafted in oak with a traditional braided paper cord seat.

Designed: 2022
Producer: Møbel Copenhagen
Materials: European oak, plywood

Rudi is a family of stackable furniture designs in wood, for both dining and lounge environments. The chair is produced in oak, with plywood for the backrest. The overall form of the chair is expressed as a series of straight lines and curves.

Rudi Chair

Dersigned: 2018
Producer: Brdr. Krüger
Materials: European oak, wool

Handcrafted by Danish furniture makers Brdr. Krüger, the Karm seating range comes in three variations, from one-seater, shown here, as well as two-, and three-seater models. The Karm one-seater is the most compact in its expression, with its frame of solid oak, and back and seat cushions upholstered in fine wool, it can stand alone as a lounge chair.

223   Karm Chair

Designed: 2018
Producer: Brdr. Krüger
Materials: European oak, wool

Like the Karm Lounge Chair (previous page), the Karm two-seater sofa, is made from large planks of natural European oak. The sofas were designed especially for the lounge at Noma.

Designed: 2018
Producer: Møbel Copenhagen
Materials: Sheepskin, polished steel

Font is a collection of upholstered chairs, sofas, lounge chairs and bar stools that are characterised by softness and comfort. Named after typeface weights, the collection includes Regular and Bold iterations, each with lightly curved backs and customised upholstery.

Font Sofa

Designed: 2018
Producer: Møbel Copenhagen
Materials: Leather, polished steel

Like the Font Sofa (previous page), the Font Regular Chair, shown here upholstered in thick pale pink leather, contrasts its plush seat and back with slender polished steel legs, giving the chair a distinctive character with a minimal presence.

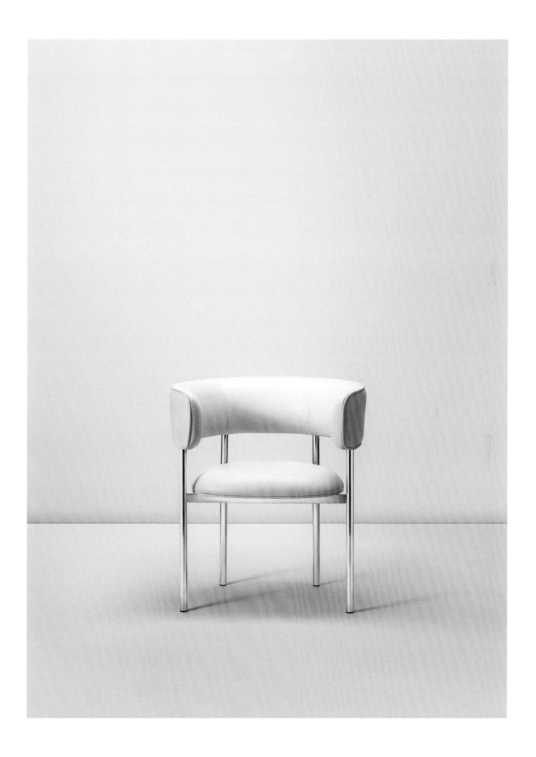

Designed: 2020
Producer: Sørensen Leather
Materials: Leather, European ash

The Landscape Divider is a cabinet supported on concealed wheels, which makes it easy to move into different locations, and to open and close. Its interior is in natural light ash with shelves that makes it possible to either leave the divider open as a display case, or closed as a tidy storage solution.

Designed: 2021
Producer: e15
Materials: Solid oak, walnut, marble, onyx

The Tore Side Tables are characterised by simple, sculptural silhouettes that are expressed in either solid oak, walnut, marble, onyx or painted in a sulphur yellow. The timeless geometric forms can be combined in different sizes and heights and arranged in a multitude of architectural compositions.

Tore Side Table

Designed: 2018
Producer: Møbel Copenhagen
Materials: Walnut, oak, granite

The Beam Table has been designed to be suitable for dining or office use, and expresses elegant structural details in the table legs and frame. Thin circular legs are made in the same wood as the tabletop, which can be produced in walnut, oak or painted finishes.

235 Beam Table

Designed: 2018
Producer: Møbel Copenhagen
Material: Polished steel, sheepskin

Like the Font Chair and Sofa (pages 224 and 226) the Font Bold Lounge Chair is named after typeface weights. The collection includes regular and bold iterations, both with lightly curved backs and customised upholstery options that have been chosen for their tactile qualities.

Font Lounge Chair

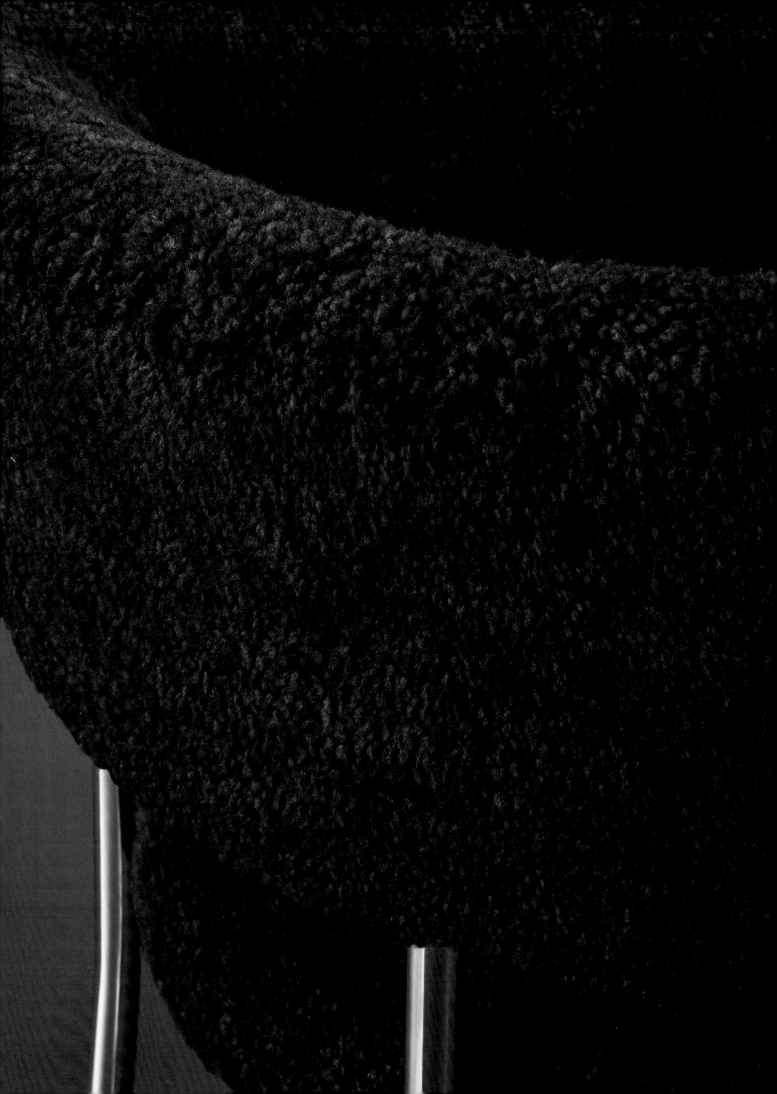

Designed: 2022
Producer: Møbel Copenhagen
Materials: Steel, ceramic

The Tile Table is inspired by 1970's Scandinavian tile coffee tables. The modular table is designed in editions of up to eight metres (26 feet) in length, which are created simply by adding more tiles. The surface is produced in a range of colours with a high-gloss glaze finish.

Tile Table

Designed: 2020
Producer: Sørensen Leather
Material: Leather, steel

The Landscape Stool is part of the same limited-edition series as the Landscape Divider and Landscape Table (pages 214 and 249) , and was inspired by classic piano stools. A simple frame of interlocking, thin steel plates surrounds a deep seat in natural leather, which together create a material and textural juxtaposition.

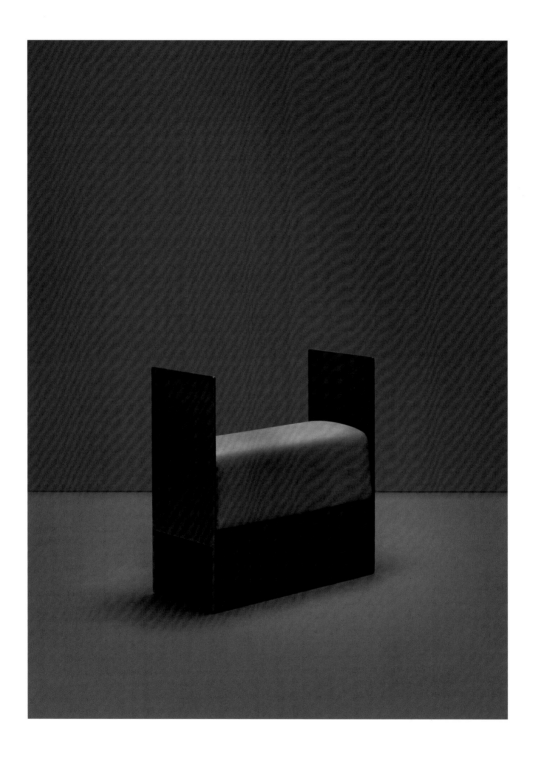

Landscape Stool

Timeline

Timeline

2009

Yde
Typology: Interior Design – Retail
Location: Copenhagen, Denmark
Client: Ole Yde

2013

Blow Hair Salon
Typology: Interior Design – Retail
Location: Copenhagen, Denmark
Client: Isabel Friis-Mikkelsen
Page 24

2014

Sturlasgade
Typology: Interior Design – Residential
Location: Copenhagen, Denmark
Client: Private

2015

Peter's House
Typology: Architecture and Interior Design – Residential
Location: Copenhagen, Denmark
Client: Peter Krasilnikoff
Page 29

Georg Jensen Copenhagen Airport
Typology: Interior Design – Retail
Location: Copenhagen, Denmark
Client: Georg Jensen

Georg Jensen Illum
Typology: Interior Design – Retail
Location: Copenhagen, Denmark
Client: Georg Jensen

Georg Jensen Oslo
Typology: Interior Design – Retail
Location: Oslo, Norway
Client: Georg Jensen

Georg Jensen Munich
Typology: Interior Design – Retail
Location: Munich, Germany
Client: Georg Jensen

Georg Jensen Manchester
Typology: Interior Design – Retail
Location: Manchester, United Kingdom
Client: Georg Jensen

Georg Jensen Westfield
Typology: Interior Design – Retail
Location: London, England, UK
Client: Georg Jensen

Georg Jensen Royal Exchange
Typology: Interior Design – Retail
Location: London, United Kingdom
Client: Georg Jensen

Georg Jensen Mount Street
Typology: Interior Design – Retail
Location: London, United Kingdom
Client: Georg Jensen

Georg Jensen Harrods
Typology: Interior Design – Retail Concept
Location: London, United Kingdom
Client: Georg Jensen

2016

Kroyers Plads
Typology: Interior Design – Residential
Location: Copenhagen, Denmark
Client: Private

Hugo Boss
Typology: Interior Design – Retail Concept
Location: Global
Client: Hugo Boss

2017

Vipp Loft
Typology: Interior Design – Residential
Location: Copenhagen, Denmark
Client: Vipp
Page 156

Hay
Typology: Interior Design – Retail
Location: Chengdu, Shanghai, Suzhou, China
Client: Hay

2018

Arv Chair
Typology: Product Design – Furniture
Manufacturer: Brdr. Krüger
Page 218

Arv Round Table & Long Table
Typology: Product Design – Furniture
Manufacturer: Brdr. Krüger

Beam Table
Typology: Product Design – Furniture
Producer: Møbel Copenhagen
Page 234

Font Chair
Typology: Product Design – Furniture
Producer: Møbel Copenhagen
Page 228

Font Lounge Chair
Typology: Product Design – Furniture
Producer: Møbel Copenhagen
Page 236

Font Sofa
Typology: Product Design – Furniture
Producer: Møbel Copenhagen
Page 227

Karm Sofa
Typology: Product Design – Furniture
Producer: Brdr. Krüger
Page 224

Collage Illum
Typology: Interior Design – Retail
Location: Copenhagen, Denmark
Client: Group 88

Collage Aarhus
Typology: Interior Design – Retail
Location: Aarhus, Denmark
Client: Group 88
Page 128

Dinesen Showroom
Typology: Interior Design – Retail
Location: Aarhus, Denmark
Client: Dinesen

J.Lindeberg
Typology: Interior Design – Retail
Location: Stockholm, Sweden
Client: J.Lindeberg
Page 116

Mooner Sofa Collection
Typology: Product Design – Furniture
Producer: Common Seating

Mark Kenly Domino Tan
Typology: Interior Design – Retail
Location: Copenhagen, Denmark
Client: Mark Kenly Domino Tan
Page 120

Noma
Typology: Interior Design – Restaurant
Location: Copenhagen, Denmark
Client: René Redzepi/Noma
Page 76

Tableau
Typology: Interior Design – Retail
Location: Copenhagen, Denmark
Client: Julius Iversen
Page 22

Wulff & Konstali
Typology: Interior Design – Restaurant
Location: Copenhagen, Denmark
Client: Wullf & Konstali

Østerbrogade 104
Typology: Interior Design – Residential
Location: Copenhagen, Denmark
Client: Private

Ary Lamp
Typology: Product Design – Lighting
Producer: XAL

Arv Lounge Chair
Typology: Product Design – Furniture
Producer: Brdr. Krüger

Momentum Collection – Low table, High Table,
Podium and Screen
Typology: Product Design – Furniture
Producer: Søuld
Page 212

Nabla Rug
Typology: Product Design – Homewares
Producer: Made By Hand

Tore Side Table
Typology: Product Design – Furniture
Producer: e15
Page 232

Tank Bar Stool
Typology: Product Design – Furniture
Producer: e15
Page 214

Jagger
Typology: Interior Design – Restaurant
Location: Copenhagen, Denmark
Client: Jagger

2022

TOG Offices
Typology: Interior Design – Workplace
Location: UK and Denmark
Client: The Office Group

Tile Table
Typology: Product Design – Furniture
Producer: Møbel Copenhagen
Page 238

Taku Seating Collection
Typology: Product Design – Furniture
Producer: Møbel Copenhagen

Rudi Chair
Typology: Product Design – Furniture
Producer: Møbel Copenhagen
Page 220

Globus Department Store
Typology: Interior Design – Retail
Location: Zurich, Switzerland
Client: Globus

Index

Acknowledgements

About the Author

A project is never carried out alone, and through the years I have learned a lot from so many people who enrich the projects I do, as well as from the conversations I have shared with passionate people in the business.

Special thanks go to Sophie Lovell, Orlando Lovell, Claus Due, Martin Nielsen, Virginia McLeod and Sarah Massey for working so hard on this book. Special thanks are also due to every collaborator and client who took the time to add their voices to, and share their knowledge about, my work, in particular: Tony Chambers, Farah Ebrahimi, Yves Marbrier, René Redzepi, Anne-Louise Sommer, and Mei and Allan Warburg.

I am equally grateful to all the collaborating photographers who, each time we document a project, keep evolving and striving for even better images, in particular: Irina Boersma, Hampus Berndtson, Peter Krasilnikoff, Jean-Francois Jaussaud and Eric Petscheck.

A tight and close team is very important for me in the successful realisation of the projects. Thank you all for your daily commitment and hard work; Antonia Fölger, Lucille Gairin, Carlotta Henrich-Bandis, Johannes Bonde, Matteo Lubelli, Sebastian Lykke-Bech, Georgina Prittie, Kristoffer Schmidt, Stefano Vito Sangirardi and Stefano Zugno. I also want to thank all past team members for their time and devotion, as well as all the amazing interns who have passed through my studio.

A very special thanks goes to all the producers, collaborators and passionate people who believed that my designs should be produced. And most importantly of all, to my clients: thank you for your trust. I never stop enjoying and learning from your dreams and aspirations!

David Thulstrup

Sophie Lovell was born in London and studied Biology at Sussex University before going on to study Design at Chelsea College of Art & Design. She moved to her current home, Berlin, in 1994. Sophie has worked on and with numerous publications both digital and analogue in the fields of art, architecture and design.

She is the former editor-in-chief of *uncube* magazine, for example, and the Germany Editor of *Wallpaper** magazine from 2000 to 2022. She has written and edited a number of books on design and architecture, including *Dieter Rams: As Little Design as Possible*, and is also co-editor of The Common Table, (the.commontable.eu) a digital platform for food futures and systemic change that she founded together with her daughter Orlando Lovell as studio_lovell.

Phaidon Press Limited
2 Cooperage Yard
London E15 2QR

Phaidon Press Inc.
65 Bleecker Street
New York, NY 10012

phaidon.com

First published 2023
© 2023 Phaidon Press Limited

ISBN 978 1 83866 631 6

A CIP catalogue record for this book is available from the British
Library and the Library of Congress.

Commissioning Editor: Virginia McLeod
Project Editors: Sarah Massey, Virginia McLeod
Production Controllers: Nerissa Vales, Lily Rodgers
Design: Studio Claus Due, Cantina

Printed in China

The publisher would like to acknowledge the invaluable contri-
butions of the following people: Vanessa Bird, James Brown,
Julia Hasting, Vishwa Kaushal, João Mota, Martin Nielsen, Rosie
Pickles and Ana Rita Teodoro.